GOD, TRUMP, and COVID-19

STEPHEN E. STRANG

FRONT LINE

PRAISE FOR
GOD, TRUMP, AND COVID-19

God, Trump, and COVID-19 is a riveting analysis of Trump's handling of the pandemic, its seismic effect on the economy, and what it could mean for every American come Election Day. Strang pulls no punches in his views on the Left, the resiliency of a president under fire, and what this all means for the US church. This book is a perfect follow-up to the author's triumvirate of books on President Trump.

—DOUG WEAD
ADVISER TO TWO PRESIDENTS AND BEST-SELLING AUTHOR

Stephen Strang's newest book presents a refreshing alternative to the fake news of today's secular media. It gives me a more accurate, faith-based understanding of Trump's handling of the pandemic and will guide my personal decision-making as we move out of this season. I highly recommend *God, Trump, and COVID-19* to anyone who wants a real view of why we need to support Trump more, not less, in the upcoming presidential election!

—CINDY JACOBS
COFOUNDER, GENERALS INTERNATIONAL

Another blockbuster book from Stephen Strang. And this one couldn't be more timely. The Latin root for the word *quarantine* is *forty*. In the Bible, from Moses to the Exodus to Jesus' fasting, when God is moving, *forty* is a key number. With quarantine virtually worldwide, this is a time when God is working in a special way. *God, Trump, and COVID-19* will give you unparalleled insights into this moment in history. Do not miss the opportunity to read this amazing book.

—PETER LOWE
CEO, ELEV8 SUMMITS

Once again my good friend Stephen Strang eloquently unfolds the true story the media fails to report. This book is a must-read for every Christian looking for biblical perspective on the COVID-19 pandemic.

—Scott Plakon
Florida State Representative, District 29

In Scripture, God used nonbelievers to accomplish His purposes. Only God knows Trump's heart, but his fruit is arguably the most pro-Christian of any president in recent history. This well-referenced book on the COVID-19 pandemic can open our eyes to the skeptics and remind us what is at stake when we vote in November. *God, Trump, and COVID-19* is a must-read book for every American, regardless of party.

—KC Craichy
Founder and CEO, Living Fuel

Steve has done it again! This sequel to *God, Trump, and the 2020 Election* is intriguing, as it draws upon Strang's unique gift to skillfully fuse careful investigative reporting with a real-time Christian perspective on God, Trump, and COVID-19.

—Frank Amedia
Founder, Touch Heaven Ministries

Stephen Strang shows why Donald Trump is the battle-tested leader we need to lead us through this spiritual and political war. In the face of this unforeseen pandemic, Trump is proving again to be the best leader for Christians and America.

—Joshua James Ford
CEO/Founder, Exaltify Media

Knowing Stephen Strang for many years, I appreciate his keen insight and prophetic understanding of what God is doing. In this book he clearly explains what is at stake in this 2020 election to equip you to share with others the importance of keeping a man in the White House who upholds Christian values.

—Pastor Eugene R. Smith
City Church

GOD, TRUMP, AND COVID-19 by Stephen E. Strang
Published by FrontLine
Charisma Media/Charisma House Book Group
600 Rinehart Road, Lake Mary, Florida 32746

Visit the author's website at charismamag.com, SteveStrangBooks.com.

Library of Congress Cataloging-in-Publication Data:
An application to register this book for cataloging has been submitted to
the Library of Congress.

International Standard Book Number: 978-1-62999-917-3
E-book ISBN: 978-1-62999-918-0

20 21 22 23 24 — 987654321
Printed in the United States of America

Most Charisma House Book Group products are available at special
quantity discounts for bulk purchase for sales promotions, premiums,
fund-raising, and educational needs. For details, call us at (407) 333-
0600 or visit our website at www.charismahouse.com.

ACKNOWLEDGMENTS

WRITING A BOOK in the midst of the COVID-19 pandemic in only nineteen days and getting it published shortly thereafter is a monumental task that took a team that I want to thank.

I deeply appreciate the collaborative editing by Todd Coconoto of Remnant News in Nashville, Tennessee, who helped flesh out my ideas in each chapter I finished as I began working on the next. Marti Pieper from North Carolina worked as an editor at Charisma Media for several years before she retired. We called her out of retirement because I knew she was a good editor. But her skill as a wordsmith and attention to detail exceeded my expectations. Both editors were fun to work with. As we worked, my friend Josh Ford of Indianapolis gave us helpful feedback chapter by chapter.

My thanks also go out to Kyle Duncan, our vice president of content development, along with his team, including Melissa Bogdany and Adrienne Gaines—they set a new land-speed record once I turned in my manuscript editing and fact-checking this book.

Finally, I appreciate Marcos Perez, executive vice president of the Charisma Media Book Group, who, like a grand maestro, directed editorial, marketing, and production to perform beautifully together to get this timely book to market in record time.

And I thank you for reading this book and for telling your friends to read it, along with the main book (to which this is a sequel), *God, Trump, and the 2020 Election*!

CONTENTS

DEDICATION

This book is dedicated to my friend Rev. Greg Mundis, of Springfield, Missouri, the executive director of Assemblies of God World Missions. He was the first person I knew personally to become ill with COVID-19, which he contracted from a group of French delegates he hosted in March. He was on a ventilator and nearly died but has survived, thanks to prayer. And to the tens of thousands of other survivors of this novel coronavirus.

IN LOVING MEMORY

The book is also dedicated in loving memory to my first personal friend to die of COVID-19—my longtime friend Bishop Phillip Brooks of Detroit. He was first assistant presiding bishop of the Church of God in Christ and succumbed to the disease on April 9, 2020. And to the tens of thousands of others who lost their lives to this dreaded disease.

FOREWORD

In *GOD, TRUMP, and COVID-19*, Stephen Strang challenges us to awaken and arise as our nation stands at a major crossroads. How will this pandemic affect the coming presidential election—and what are God's prophets saying in this critical time?

Even before the decimating effects of the coronavirus swept around the world, God was warning us—His church—that He had extended His hand of mercy on America and had withheld judgment for our decades-long slide into moral relativism and the loss of biblical values.

As Stephen points out in his previous book, *God, Trump, and the 2020 Election*, though Donald Trump is as imperfect as any of us, God has raised him up to stand up for many biblical principles—including the life of the unborn (a cause very dear to my heart) as well as the protection of our right to worship as a church.

Now, however, whether you think the pandemic is simply a result of living in a fallen world, or it is indeed God's wrath, our response *must* be the same: to rise up as the church, put away childish and trivial things, and step into our place as the Lord's remnant on earth. This book is an excellent clarion call that does just that!

Like a watchman sounding the alarm from atop our city walls, Steve uses his years of journalistic expertise to warn us of enemies approaching—and scaling—our gates. The enemy is a God-hating, life-mocking, Jesus-dismissing spirit represented in continuing attacks by many in secular positions of power who would like nothing more than to see America become a truly post-Christian nation.

People, let us *not* remain asleep during this time to *act*. As God's people, we must press in now more than ever before to pray for the peace of Jerusalem, for our president, and for a great harvest of souls. *Now* more than anytime in the past century God has the world's attention. Let us heed the advice so expertly presented in these pages and arise, for the glory of God.

—Lori Bakker
Author, Speaker, and
Cohost of *The Jim Bakker Show*

Introduction

FOR SUCH A TIME AS THIS

THE NOVEL CORONAVIRUS, which originated in Wuhan, China, will likely be remembered similarly to the way we recall Pearl Harbor or September 11, 2001. In some ways America will never be the same, and I knew I needed to deal with this by writing a quick update of my book *God, Trump, and the 2020 Election*. I completed that book in the fall of 2019, and it was released January 14, 2020—around the time news reports out of China were warning of a new virus infecting many.

Fast-forward to April 2020, when I felt compelled to put together this book—call it part 2 of the *God, Trump, and the 2020 Election* message—which I wrote in less than two weeks. Even though you may be reading this after the main threat of the novel coronavirus has passed, I trust that these chapters will help you better understand the events and issues that have changed us irrevocably.

Thankfully, President Trump had quickly shut down the US borders, announcing on January 31 travel restrictions on those coming from China, effective February 2, and then, effective March 16, on those coming from Europe, where the virus was spreading quickly. He declared the outbreak a national emergency on March 13.

At the time, there was sharp criticism from Democrats, most notably Joe Biden, who condemned "Trump's record of hysteria, xenophobia, and fear-mongering" after he announced the China travel restrictions.[1] Trump said Democrats "loudly criticized and protested"[2] his travel restrictions and that Biden "called me a racist" because of the decision.[3]

Trump may have slightly overstated the Democratic opposition's position. But according to *The Hill*, on January 31, 2020, Speaker of the House Nancy Pelosi said President Trump's decision to extend the travel ban to six African nations was "outrageous, un-American and threatened the rule of law."[4] That statement didn't age well. In addition, the World Health Organization (WHO) tweeted on January 14 that there was no clear evidence of human-to-human transmission of the virus, but by January 23 the organization said human-to-human transmission was occurring.

However, President Trump, whose keen leadership instincts told him to take these actions even as the impeachment farce was wrapping up with his acquittal in the Senate on February 5, was taking action to protect the American people—putting them first. In predictable style the Left and the mainstream media blasted him as an alarmist. Of course, when things got really bad, they changed their tune. After all, the strong Trump economy began to plummet, and companies were shuttered—especially businesses that dealt with the public, such as restaurants and hairdressers. Even most churches closed their doors after March 16, when the president released guidelines recommending gatherings be limited to no more than ten people.

Even with the stay-at-home orders, some enterprises were considered essential—drugstores and grocery stores, for example. Restaurants and bars had to close except for takeout or delivery. However, churches were considered nonessential, while liquor stores were considered essential! Early reports showed that liquor sales were way up while people sheltered in place.

This created an interesting question about religious liberty. Why did the government bureaucrats consider churches nonessential? We do, after all, have a constitutional right to freedom of religion.

Rodney Howard Browne, pastor of the megachurch The River at

Tampa Bay in Florida, held services after sanitizing everything and making sure people stayed the required six feet apart. The sheriff of his county held a press conference to shame Pastor Howard-Browne for disregarding public safety and announced a warrant for his arrest had been issued, and later deputies went to his home to arrest him on two second-degree misdemeanors.

Liberty Counsel pointed out that Americans have freedom of religion under the Constitution, but many businesses allowed to stay open, such as The Home Depot or repair shops, have no such right. After being threatened with a constitutional lawsuit they knew they would lose, the local Hillsborough County authorities changed and said churches were essential. Florida governor Ron DeSantis and several other governors determined that churches were essential in their states. In a way, religious liberty won. But if it's a virus this time, what happens next time officials order churches to close, especially after so many have quietly gone along with the shutdown orders?

The coronavirus has changed everything. Someday the virus itself will be contained or prevented. But millions of people have discovered they don't have to rush around. Staying at home with the family isn't that bad. And even President Trump said watching church online—which he said he has done several Sundays during the shutdown—wasn't so bad.

The coronavirus has also changed our politics. The Left already wants the government to do everything and pay for everything. Now even conservatives seem to like the Paycheck Protection Program, through which the government basically pays businesses to keep their workers on the payroll.

For a couple of weeks normal politics were on the back burner— no political rallies. Joe Biden was in his basement giving video news conferences to try to stay relevant but making gaffes and bumbling his words, even when a friendly journalist tried to help him.

Most of the news focused on the coronavirus instead of endless investigations and impeachment. Even Gov. Gavin Newsome of California and Gov. Andrew Cuomo of New York had nice things to say about President Trump when he rushed to their aid as the pandemic hit those states particularly hard. But the Democrats also blasted him for acting too slowly. Nancy Pelosi said people would die because of Trump's incompetence as a leader.

But the opposite was true. In one debate Bernie Sanders and Joe Biden both said they would not have closed the borders. Of course not; they are *for* open borders. Ironically our southern border finally closed when officials figured out that illegal immigrants pouring across the border might be bringing COVID-19 into the country.

Several prominent Democrats, such as Nancy Pelosi, said Americans didn't need to panic about the virus. Fox News host Jesse Watters called the Democrats out on this during a recent broadcast, saying, "Not too long ago, Cuomo was saying go eat out in New York City. [Bill] de Blasio had all of the schools open. Nancy Pelosi said bring your friends to Chinatown and go to the bars. Joe Biden said the travel ban was racist."[5] Most of the media neglect to replay these sound bites.

I believe Donald Trump has given great leadership in this pandemic. I believe he will continue to give great leadership and the economy will roar back. As bad as the pandemic is, it may help him to win even bigger in the November election. But all bets are off. Trump's single major selling point to American voters who normally might not vote for a Republican was the soaring economy. The *New York Post* reported on March 21: "The coronavirus poses an 'existential threat' to President Donald Trump's 2020 re-election, campaign insiders and GOP operatives say."[6] If this is true, then we have even more reason to back this president and help him get reelected.

Why did I write this book on such short notice? It's an important subject I'm interested in. And of course the public is interested. This also ties in with my book *God, Trump, and the 2020 Election*. I wanted to make the case that Trump is providing good leadership through this, which is one more reason we must return him to office.

But even more importantly, I want the reader to understand where God is in the midst of a historically tense, intense time. And I felt the need to tell the untold story of what the prophets are saying and unpack what that means, including where they were right and what this means for the future of America and the church.

I've written several books about Donald Trump because I believe we are at a critical juncture in the life of our country, and I believe God has raised up this incredible leader for such a time as this. My previous book, *God, Trump, and the 2020 Election*, explores what is at stake if he loses in November. It is the most important book I've ever written. If you haven't read it, I hope you will—not because it's my book but because I believe it will help *you* understand what the liberal fake news (and even the more conservative secular news media) won't tell you: Where is God in all this, and what is His will?

God, Trump, and the 2020 Election has done very well and is getting good reviews, but a month after it was released in January 2020, the first case of COVID-19 was discovered in the United States. In a matter of weeks everything changed. In early April I felt I should write a new book about how this unexpected pandemic could affect the outcome of this election. It's much shorter than my other books, and I wrote it in only nineteen days. It's timely and topical and in some ways is the sequel to *God, Trump, and the 2020 Election*.

I know many readers have read it, and maybe that's why you decided to read what else I have written about this important time in American history, leading up to the most important election in our lifetimes. If you have not read *God, Trump, and the 2020 Election*, I hope you enjoy this book and that it makes you want to read the original. Not only did I have a chapter in that book on "Why Trump Must Win," but I had a chapter on "Why He Might Lose." One of the reasons was if something terrible were to happen to the economy. In late 2019 when I wrote that chapter, it seemed to me that the economy would continue to soar. Now all that has changed. And it might affect the outcome of the election.

Soon the pandemic will end and our country will return to some form of new normal. And when November 3 rolls around, we will have an election, no matter what. The issues about freedom and religious liberty and how desperate (and frankly dishonest) the Left is will still be with us. If anything, the stakes will be even higher than if this pandemic hadn't happened.

Most readers know I'm a publisher—it's how I make a living. But I wrote these books not just to sell books but to light a fire under the Christian community that we must turn out at the polls like never before, or life as we know it will end and persecution of Christians and those who oppose the Leftist agenda will likely begin.

You can decide if I make the case well. If I do, I hope you will encourage others to read not only this small book but the original as well. Once the supply chain opens up again, it will be available wherever books are sold. Plus, you can get it online, including on our website SteveStrangBooks.com. I hope you read it, recommend it, and become passionate about reelecting a president raised up by God for such a time as this.

Bible-believing voters—whether Democrats, Independents, or

Republicans—do have some key nonnegotiables that usually impact their voting:

- Protection of religious liberties and freedoms
- Nomination of Supreme Court candidates who will base decisions on a constructionist view of the Constitution (i.e., not activist judges)
- Protection of the unborn
- Support of Israel
- Determination to stop the persecution of Christians and religious minorities around the world

Evangelicals typically agree on these key issues (which I documented in *God, Trump, and the 2020 Election*).

Things were so desperate when Hillary Clinton was running for president that the American people took a chance on a political outsider. After the coronavirus has passed us, we will need the leadership of this dynamic president to help our country get back to normal. And come what may, there will be an election on November 3, and we cannot allow Joe Biden to be elected for all the reasons I outline in *God, Trump, and the 2020 Election*.

—Stephen Strang
Longwood, Florida
April 22, 2020

Chapter 1

THE PLAGUE THAT NOW AFFECTS THE 2020 ELECTION

I see a plague coming on the world and the bars, church, and government shut down. The plague will hit New York City and shake it like it has never been shaken. The plague is going to force prayerless believers into radical prayer, into their Bibles and repentance will be the cry from true men of God in the pulpit. And out of it will come a third Great Awakening that will sweep America and the world.[1]

THIS 1986 PROPHECY by late Christian leader and author David Wilkerson (which I discuss later in this book) describes perfectly what we now call the COVID-19 pandemic. How could he have known, and how might this current crisis spark a Third Great Awakening? Is it possible God is up to something? I believe Donald Trump has shown great leadership in this crisis—but what does this mean for the 2020 election?

When I finished *God, Trump, and the 2020 Election* in October 2019, there was no way of knowing that a pandemic was coming. COVID-19 had not yet been discovered. And no one anticipated the global crisis that was poised to strike. China tried to cover it up for several months and even arrested the doctors who sounded the alarm.[2] Then, the crowds of visitors for Chinese New Year took the virus back home until the pandemic spread around the world. At that time, no one could have fathomed how this would develop into a 9/11-level event that will most likely forever change the way we conduct business and trade, interact socially, and so much more.

Yet back in December—before people all over China began falling sick with pneumonia-like symptoms, before people around the world grew alarmed about a disease, and before the coronavirus reached new shores after being carried onto planes by human hosts, forcing the WHO to declare a global emergency—eight whistleblowers were already discussing how several patients in Wuhan were experiencing severe, rapid breakdowns in their respiratory systems.

These whistleblowers were part of a medical school's alumni group on WeChat, a popular social network in China, and they were concerned that severe acute respiratory syndrome (SARS) had returned. If not SARS, perhaps the threat came from something similar of unknown origin.

It wasn't long before Chinese police detained these eight doctors and medical technicians. Authorities said they were "misinforming" the public, that there was no SARS, that the information was obviously wrong, and that everyone in the city must remain calm. On the first day of 2020, Wuhan police said they had "taken legal measures" against the eight individuals who had "spread rumors."[3] We will dig into this in more detail later on.

God, Trump, and the 2020 Election documents how Donald Trump stood up to the radical Left, supported traditional values such as life for the unborn, and in many ways exposed the evil by the entrenched bureaucracy we now call the Deep State. The Democrats and their allies in the press also opposed him at every turn, including the two-year Mueller investigation, which showed no wrongdoing, and even tried to impeach him. Meanwhile the economy was booming, and the president was making America great again by actually keeping his promises to strengthen the economy, cut onerous regulations that stifle business, and look out for the little guy. Now, because of a virtual shutdown of the country due to the novel coronavirus, which causes COVID-19, everything has changed.

Renowned economist Stephen Moore originally felt bullish on how the economy would "roar back"[4] after the Coronavirus Task Force implemented its initial "15 days to slow the spread" nationwide. But as the shutdown was extended to forty-five days, Moore[5] and other economic experts, such as Mark Skausen, began to sound the alarm about long-term devastation that might result if both small businesses and large corporations were limited to operating in a virtual environment. The same would be true if nonessential retailers were forced to rely strictly on online sales. One thing is certain: the COVID-19 pandemic has affected everything in the economy.

But one thing that hasn't changed is Donald Trump is a leader, and at this point in American history we need a real leader who can get private enterprise and government—and even the Democrats—to work together to take us through this crisis and find a vaccine for this deadly virus. Remember how feckless Jimmy Carter was with the Iran hostage situation,[6] and even the way George W. Bush didn't seem to know how to crush al Qaeda[7] after 9/11.

In contrast, Trump quickly closed travel from China[8] and later from Europe[9] even though liberals accused him of overreacting and being xenophobic. In fact, both Bernie Sanders and Joe Biden[10] publicly said they would have left the borders open. Others went so far as to label the president as "racist" once again for singling out China. The mainstream media, in sound bite after sound bite, mocked his decision to be cautious, labeling it as an "extreme measure."

But before long most countries were closing their borders,[11] and the president's decisions not only proved right but may have been a determining factor as to why the United States did not see the kind of numbers of those infected with COVID-19 the original models were projecting. In fact, those numbers were lowered[12] three times. And even the southern border was finally closed[13] when officials realized the hordes of illegal immigrants who bring in various diseases could also be carrying the dreaded coronavirus.

God, Trump, and the 2020 Election contained an entire chapter on "Promises Made, Promises Kept." Here are a few of Trump's major accomplishments, many of which were detailed in that chapter, for which all Americans should be incredibly thankful:

- securing the borders and ports of entry
- being proactive in taking key precautions in the early stages of the COVID-19 outbreak despite criticism from the Left
- diversifying our supply chain and emphasizing to US companies the need to look to countries other than just China to fulfill our manufacturing needs
- renegotiating trade deals to level set and protect US financial interests
- deregulating key segments of the US manufacturing and farming sectors

If the president had not proactively done each of these things, we would be in a much worse situation than we are right now from both a health and an economic standpoint. The biased media rarely reports any of this.

Time will tell how all this plays out. The prophets have said America will bounce back more quickly than the naysayers predict. But we can be sure of three things: the pandemic is less extensive, the response is stronger, and we will get back to normal faster because we have a real leader in the White House.

It's as if we're in a war different from but no less difficult than what England faced in World War II when Winston Churchill (a leader many in England didn't like) became the instrument God used to rally the nation, help win the war, and save Western civilization from Nazism. Trump has described himself as a "wartime president,"[14] and his statement has proved true as he leads our battle with an unseen enemy.

Most Evangelicals believe our nation was founded on a love for God and reverence for His Word, and because of that we have experienced His undeserved favor upon our country. Even in the midst of this COVID-19 pandemic, God comforts, protects, and brings the truth to light, giving us hope and peace during periods of uncertainty, fear, and upset.

I've written extensively that I believe God raised up Donald Trump to help turn things around in America, and I believe in many ways he has done just that. I make the case that much of this has taken place because Trump is such a strong leader and because God seems to have His hand on this billionaire from Queens who won the presidency against all odds.

I believe Donald Trump is in the right place at the right time to lead the country through this unprecedented pandemic. Even though I finished writing *God, Trump, and the 2020 Election* months before we learned of the coronavirus, I believe the case I make for Donald Trump is still valid as the nation reels from the effects of this virus on both the health of individuals and the economy—indeed, on our very nation.

Something incredible happened in the White House only days before Easter this year. On Good Friday, President Donald Trump held a service in the Oval Office. I call it a service because the things he said were pointing people back to God in this tumultuous time. Once he was done speaking, he turned the service over to Bishop Harry R. Jackson, senior pastor of Hope Christian Church in Beltsville, Maryland, and presiding bishop of the International Communion of Evangelical Churches. Bishop Jackson is also an adviser to Trump and a good friend of mine. He took that time to pray for a blessing over our president and over our nation.

It was refreshing to see such a spiritual moment in the Oval Office. You can watch the event on YouTube.[15] In a podcast I did with Bishop Jackson recently, he told me he was humbled to be up there with the president praying. He said Trump asked him at one point if he ever gets nervous praying and speaking in front of people. Bishop Jackson replied yes, to which Trump responded, "But you don't look nervous."

Bishop Jackson explained that he wasn't nervous about what people would think of him—he simply felt the weight of what his prayer could do to shift things in the spiritual realm.

"We as Christians believe that prayer changes things. We believe that although God's in control of everything…He has given an opportunity for us to, in a sense, influence the future destiny of a nation, the destiny of our families."

Bishop Jackson told me, "So I was humbled by that. And I took comfort in knowing that God would give this man in the greatest office in the land, and Vice President [Mike] Pence—He would give them both wisdom."[16]

Bishop Jackson believes prayer is especially vital right now, with the COVID-19 pandemic raging. A few weeks ago he received a revelation that prayer was going to impact the nation's destiny. He was reading in Numbers 16, where God sent a plague to the people of Israel because a group was rebelling against Moses and Aaron.

Moses knew the plague had occurred because of the people's rebellion, so he told Aaron to run and grab his censer—which Bishop Jackson said represents the prayers of the saints—and stand "between the dead and the living" (Num. 16:48).

When Aaron did that, God stopped the plague and showed mercy to Israel.

"Many national prophetic figures got that same Scripture," Bishop Jackson said. "Many of us have believed that God is going to mitigate the impact of the plague if the church prays. Ironically, from [April 10, Good] Friday at noon to Monday and Tuesday [April 14] at noon, all of a sudden we found the governor talking about the fact that everything had peaked in New York. And it seemed as though our Passover prayer—asking God to pass over, asking God to use our prayers to be like Aaron's incense, forming a line between the living and the dead—actually worked."

Bishop Jackson reiterated that it wasn't his prayer, or anyone's prayer specifically, that changed the tide of the coronavirus deaths. But rather it was God's mercy in response to His people's cries.

And more of God's mercy is certainly on its way. Bishop Jackson believes God is stirring up awakening in this season.

"I believe that we're going to see evangelism at its best manifest in this season," he says. "I'm excited about it. And awakening is at the door, following the shaking, so that our confidence might not be in the arm of the flesh but in the Word of the living God."[17]

Chapter 2

SUPPORTING THE PRESIDENT IN HIS BIGGEST CHALLENGE

IT'S IRONIC AND hypocritical that many on the Left have been so desperate to criticize President Donald Trump in his quest of making America great again. For example, in his handling of the COVID-19 crisis, the criticisms were wide and varied: Trump didn't close the borders soon enough; he closed them too soon. He didn't speak up enough; he spoke up too much. He took the advice of the wrong people; he didn't listen to enough people.

Even before the COVID-19 pandemic, liberals criticized President Trump for everything from his lifestyle—although before he ran for president as a Republican, they saw nothing wrong with his past and he seemed to be the darling of the liberal media—to his beliefs. Has he done and said things that don't reflect the teachings of the Bible? Yes. He's imperfect, but according to some, that makes him a great leader.

In the same way, some Christians overlook the good Trump has done and focus on all the mistakes he's made and the perceived weaknesses he still struggles with. The question we must ask ourselves, though, is, What is the fruit? Donald Trump has probably been one of the staunchest defenders of religious liberties and freedoms we have seen. He also makes it no secret that he has an evangelical council that meets with him periodically, ministers to him, advises him, and at times even lays hands on and prays over him.

"As Christians we have created artificial standards for our leaders that God doesn't have for His leaders in the Bible," historian

David Barton told me for *God, Trump, and the 2020 Election*. "I have flaws, Trump has flaws, and we can point them out in a self-righteous manner. Or we can look at Hebrews 11 and see that all these great leaders had serious flaws but God definitely still used them."

Barton said conservative Christians should "look at what the president has done for the economy, but especially standing for religious liberty, appointing righteous judges, protecting unborn life, and supporting Israel—so many of the things the Bible specifically talks about. No president in our lifetime has gotten done as many biblically correct things as he has."

Because of this, Barton said Christians must be willing to support Trump and not allow the Left to undermine his conservative agenda any longer. He points out that we don't have to win every American to our way of thinking—we just need to win more than we have now.

Author Lance Wallnau has made the same point. "Figures like Churchill, Lincoln, and George S. Patton don't step out of cathedrals onto the stage of history, yet we canonize them later as instruments God raised up to meet a singular crisis," he said.[1] None of these men were conventional Christians, and they had many detractors in the clergy, yet each played a pivotal role in history. They stood strong against the enemies of freedom and helped safeguard our way of life and Christian heritage.

History has shown that Winston Churchill was the right man at the right time to be used by God, yet he was also unpopular. In fact, Churchill was described with terms often used in association with Donald Trump. Critics called him an "'aristocratic adventurer' who lacked good judgment and political skills." He was considered "rootless…unstable…unsound…an undeniable cad," according to the biography *God and Churchill: How the Great Leader's Sense of Divine Destiny Changed His Troubled World and Offers Hope for Ours* by Churchill's great-grandson the late Jonathan Sandys and Wallace Henley. Churchill was "an embarrassment" to important people in the Conservative Party. And he was viewed as impetuous—"'a real danger' who…tended not to count the cost of his endeavors."[2]

The British didn't like him until they needed someone strong enough to defeat the Nazis. Churchill didn't have many fans within the Christian community, either. The conservative Christians of the day in Britain didn't like the fact that he smoked cigars and loved drinking brandy. Churchill was a deeply flawed man, but God still raised him up to save Western civilization.

Churchill seemed to know this. Sandys asserts that his famous great-grandfather felt a call from God his entire life that he was to save Western civilization. A case can be made, of course, that Churchill did just that when he stopped Hitler from taking over Great Britain. In the face of Hitler's military might, Churchill had to resolve to move ahead anyhow and to never quit. Churchill was a strong leader, and his example shows that God uses whomever He chooses.

That's what I see in Donald Trump and why people support him despite all the criticisms thrown at him. In that respect Trump resembles the indefatigable British prime minister, who often went against convention, decorum, and his own party to badger the people of Great Britain into defending their country against Hitler's Third Reich. Churchill was viciously attacked by the media in his day. Today, Donald Trump invites the same kinds of bitterness and resentment by raising alarms about the unraveling of American society at a time when our political elites, buttressed by the media, are denying that anything is wrong. Like Churchill, Trump is the target of opposition forces seeking to silence him for his bluntness and to stop him from speaking from the heart about problems the political establishment has been sweeping under the carpet for generations.

True leaders such as Churchill show strength of character in the face of adversity. Granted, Britain was in a life-and-death struggle with Nazi Germany, which threatened to destroy all of civilization. Forgive me if this seems hyperbolic, but the situation today in America is almost as serious, considering the world we might have entered had Hillary Clinton won the election instead of Trump. It's a world where we could have lost our constitutional protections of our religious freedoms. In this case our struggle wasn't with guns, tanks, and planes; it was a political battle over the presidency and the direction of our nation now and for generations.

Although some people interpreted Donald Trump's win as a political revolution, many conservative Christians saw it as a cultural counter-revolution and an answer to prayer. Evangelist and media personality James Robison told me that in 2016 "a lot of Christians were praying that we wouldn't lose freedom, that we would not lose the opportunities this nation offers with the protections and safeguards, and government functioning as a protector, and not potentially replacing God and our love for one another."

Robison, who serves on the president's Faith Advisory Board and remains a friend and confidant of Trump's, believes now that Donald Trump represents a supernatural answer to prayer, but he didn't come in the package people wanted. Of the seventeen Republican nominees, he ranked as the last choice of most Evangelicals. "He would have been my last choice," Robison told me. "Many conservatives said that we don't know where Donald Trump is going to end up taking us, but we know exactly where Hillary Clinton would take us, and that would be a continuation of everything that's wrong, destructive, and that would ruin America by taking away our freedoms."

The secular pundits saw Trump's victory only as a battle between Democrat and Republican, or between the Left and the Right. But Robison saw it as a supernatural spiritual battle. "What happened," he told me, "is that God overpowered the foolishness of political correctness and the liberal (not just deceived but possessed) Left, which is far too often dead set against a biblical worldview and against America's traditional Judeo-Christian ethics. But they were being totally pushed back."

The secular Left in this country, Robison said, are being manipulated by the powers Jesus was talking about when He said of those who crucified Him, "They don't know what they are doing" (Luke 23:34, NLT). They knew exactly what they were doing, but Jesus said no, they didn't. "They were under the control of another force, another power in the invisible supernatural realm of the Spirit. They were deceived by the deceiver," Robison told me.

Millions of Christians were praying for that deception to be overthrown to prevent the government from being raised up as another form of Pharaoh or some kind of overseeing Caesar. The people were praying, "God, we've got to let You be God. We've got to stop this nonsense." And Robison added, "Christians were praying for this to be stopped, but they never dreamed that it would be some person totally disconnected with politics, totally unable to even express himself like a politician, and someone who was best known as a shrewd maneuverer."

Trump spoke with conviction about what's wrong in this country, Robison told me. "He was totally open about everything that was wrong. Most of us would agree that he didn't address those problems in the most statesmanlike or diplomatic terms, but everything he was saying was right on track. He was saying that many things in this country are bad and they needed to be dealt with. And he was 100 percent correct."

Christians who were concerned about "government masquerading as God," to use Robison's expression, knew the government needed to be brought under control, so Trump's win served as evidence that their prayers were being answered.

"He understood what it means to lay a foundation," Robison said. "He is a builder. What he didn't realize was that he was actually returning to the foundation of our freedom, and we know that the solid rock upon which we are to build is the transforming truth Jesus referred to when He said, 'You shall know the truth, and the truth shall make you free'" (John 8:32, NKJV).

Along with many other evangelical leaders, Robison initially backed Ted Cruz. But he also knew several other presidential contenders, including Rand Paul, Carly Fiorina, and his lifelong friend Rick Perry. He has prayed with all of them. "They all looked like they had such great qualifications," he said, "and frankly I was astounded that Donald Trump was even being considered and gaining momentum."

After dropping out of the race, Mike Huckabee was the first to tell Robison to get behind Trump. Robison had been recruiting Huckabee to counsel Cruz, but the governor told him, "James, the man who listens to counsel the best of anybody I've been around is Donald Trump."

Surprised to hear that, Robison said, "Mike, have you lost your mind?"

"No, I haven't. I've known him, James. I've watched him, and I know it sounds crazy, but I believe he's the right man at this time," Huckabee replied. Robison remembers hearing Jerry Falwell Jr. saying much the same thing.

After Ben Carson dropped out of the race, Robison prayed with him nearly every day on the phone. "The week that Dr. Carson decided to endorse Trump, we probably talked on average about two hours a day," Robison told me. "Then all of a sudden he told me, 'I'm endorsing Donald Trump.' And I said, 'Ben, you've lost your mind! What are you doing?' He said, 'James, listen to me. I've spent two hours with him this week and two hours another day. It's just not the way it looks.' So I asked him, 'What do you mean?' And Ben Carson told me, 'James, I'm telling you, he'll listen to wisdom. And my endorsement comes with the assurance that he will be willing to listen to those who have deep convictions and the ability to communicate their importance, and he agreed to do that.'"

Apparently Trump did listen. Before long Robison was flying with him to campaign events, giving him advice, and offering spiritual counsel whenever possible. Robison said he has met with several presidents. "None of them were as open as Donald Trump," he told me. "Mr. Trump called frequently on his cell phone, and he took my calls. We were able to have very open, honest exchanges where I could share the real concerns of pro-family, pro-faith leaders. He was always very appreciative and responsive. I was also able to travel with him on the plane and ride with him in the car in very important moments when I shared serious, deep concerns we had, which many thought Donald Trump would not listen to or even consider. But not only did he hear me with graciousness; he was very expressive in his appreciation for me and love for my family."

In an interview for *The Stream*, Robison asked Jack Graham, pastor of the nearly forty-five-thousand-member Prestonwood Baptist Church based in Plano, Texas, how he assessed the president's attitude toward people of faith. Robison said, "You've seen him in settings where someone is sharing their concern....Do you find it amazing the way this president responds to people no matter who they are?"

Graham answered, "Beyond just personal skills, I am convinced he has a genuine spiritual interest and a desire to hear the viewpoint of others. In particular, it's apparent he wants to know what conservative, Bible-believing Christians think. It's been very gratifying and satisfying. And not only him but the people he has put into place. Vice President [Mike] Pence is a great Christian. Eight or nine of his Cabinet members, the people closest to him, are Christians, and they are having Bible study and prayer together."

Graham also said, "I am grateful this president has given us the opportunity to speak into his life. When we prayed for him in the Oval Office earlier this week, though he was under a great deal of pressure, he was buoyant and joyful. We stayed in there for a good while conversing and praying. It was a God moment and a powerful experience."[3] Robison and Graham agreed that Trump's words and actions indicate that this president values the opinions of the Christian leaders.

Not only did the sudden groundswell of support for Trump occur at Trump's political rallies, but you could see it in churches, in prayer groups, and at rallies of all sorts. Cindy Jacobs, cofounder of Generals International and the Reformation Prayer Network, is not well known in evangelical circles but is widely respected by Charismatics as a prophet and teacher. She mobilized ten thousand intercessors to "prayer-walk" the seven critical states that helped Trump win in November 2016. These men and women walked around courthouses or the centers of towns praying for righteousness to prevail. In addition, a coalition of prayer leaders called As One also mobilized its networks two different times to prayer-walk for forty days.

Jacobs has ministered all over the world, and as the campaign grew more intense in the fall of 2016, she began receiving calls from friends in Europe, China, and Latin America saying intercessors were praying fervently that Trump would be elected. Many took the election so seriously they told her they were fasting and praying for hours each day. Jacobs' close friend Lou Engle, a revivalist and cofounder of TheCall, a group that hosted twelve-hour prayer rallies, urged supporters to begin a three-day fast as a petition for God's mercy. He rallied thousands to join him because things looked so bleak. Conservative Christians believed that if Hillary Clinton won this election, it would be "game over" for religious freedom.

The night before the election, Jerry Johnson, then president of National Religious Broadcasters, attended a prayer meeting in Washington, DC, and came away telling friends he believed Trump would win. I had been praying too, and I felt a similar optimism. That's why I accepted an invitation from Darrell Scott, pastor of the New Spirit Revival Center in Cleveland Heights, Ohio, to fly to New York to watch the election returns at the New York Hilton on election night. Scott was joined by several other African American pastors. That event, with the whole world watching, turned out to be a huge victory celebration. For part of the evening I stood near Pastor Robert Jeffress of First Baptist Church in Dallas. He told me what a miracle he thought it would be if Trump actually won.

For most of the evening, the television commentators kept predicting that Clinton would be victorious. Even Fox News, which was broadcast live on TV screens in the Hilton ballroom, was reporting that Clinton had the edge and Trump had too much ground to make up. Yet by 10:00 p.m. Eastern time it seemed to me that Trump's lead in electoral votes would be enough so that even a surge of West Coast victories couldn't make up the difference.

The networks were showing all of the jubilation from the Hilton ballroom. It was packed with people who had worked diligently for the campaign. Then, when Trump's numbers hit the 270 mark, the liberal commentators were stunned into silence by the realization that Trump had actually won.

Where I was standing in the Hilton ballroom, my Christian friends were shouting, and a few shed tears of joy. It was as if God had answered our prayers and the impossible had happened. We had a new president, one we believed God had raised up for such a time as this. And perhaps best of all, we each thanked God in our own way that Hillary Clinton was not going to be the next commander in chief.

Chapter 3

CHINA'S ROLE IN THE PANDEMIC

B Y FEBRUARY 13, 2020, this coronavirus, which causes COVID-19, had officially resulted in over sixty thousand proven infections, with more than thirteen hundred deaths.[1] The true numbers were without a doubt much higher, as many died at home with no report made to the authorities, and the numbers exponentially increased before the virus was brought under control. It is important to note that there have been reports that some deaths recorded as coronavirus deaths were not tested and could potentially be unrelated.

President Trump had just banned travel from China on January 31, and the news networks, which had been saying the coronavirus wasn't all that bad, were beginning to say it was worse in China than authorities were reporting.

Then, out of the blue, my longtime friend Frank Amedia sent me a text that shocked me. I knew him to be well connected with ministries around the world (I met him in Jerusalem) and laser focused on current events. He has given me some scoops in the past. He now had new information from one of his Chinese friends that on the surface sounded like a major conspiracy theory. Basically he believed he had solid proof that the virus didn't come from a wet market, as reports said at the time, but from a Wuhan virology lab that collected hundreds of viruses with the idea of finding vaccines or learning enough to prevent another SARS or swine flu outbreak.

There was speculation the military wanted to use it for biological warfare, but that may be a conspiracy theory. Something went very wrong, and the virus escaped. There are now reports that the US military was warning that the bio lab in China had weak security mechanisms. He even had the name of the scientist who leaked the news. Frank's report said the Chinese Communist Party was covering up this proof.

Frank wanted to release the information to the press and wanted to do it through Charisma News. Now, we love scoops on Charisma News. But we mostly report what is happening spiritually—news secular media won't cover. We avoid anything that sounds like a conspiracy theory and as a result have a reputation as careful, factual journalists. At the time, we had no way of knowing if this was true or how to verify it.

Frank's text is explosive, detailed, and interesting. I believe it has the ring of authenticity, but I asked Frank where he got this information. He said it came from a friend he calls Jay. He gave me Jay's number, and I called him. In his broken English, Jay verified what he had told Frank. But how could I check what he said? Wuhan, China, is a long way off. And even if we had someone there who spoke the language, how would we get past all the governmental attempts to cover up the truth?

In February, Jay said the coronavirus "plague" was completely out of control due to a lack of transparency.

He began by telling me how the outbreak had started. At the time, the official word from China and the World Health Organization was that the virus was controllable and could not be passed from human to human. At the same time, many in Wuhan were already dead or dying, but the government issued no quarantine until much later. Indeed, the quarantine order came on January 20, presumably because President Xi Jinping wanted to give the impression to the public that "everything was stable and calm." They even told people as the Chinese New Year approached that there was no reason to wear masks in public.

In early February, Jay was saying the coronavirus "plague" was completely out of control due to a lack of transparency. He told me things we now assume are true but at the time seemed pretty far-fetched. I have written about some of these elsewhere in this book. It was interesting to me that this came from a Chinese American Christian who was getting his information from the "grass roots" in China via the internet, and much of it was contradicting what we were hearing in the media at the time.

Then came the part that sounded like a conspiracy theory, and I didn't know how to confirm it:

- A secret P4 (or level 4) lab already knew this virus could be transmitted from human to human, but this fact was never disclosed.

- Corruption was exposed in late January involving the government and the Red Cross in Wuhan, which had collected more than five hundred million ¥ (Chinese currency), but none was distributed. Some officials in the Red Cross were removed from their posts after this scandal was publicized on a website, Jay said.

- The Communist Party officials said the outbreak of the virus started at a seafood (wet) market, which was imme- diately scrubbed, washing away any crucial evidence. "Typical Communist Party act," Jay said.

- However, the first person infected had never been to that market, and of the first forty-one people who were infected, Jay said one-third of them never went to that market. Most of the rest never ate bats or snakes during that period of time. "This finding almost rules out the possibility of the original source of this plague," Jay wrote.

- In the meantime, many scientists also suspected China's P4 lab (the top chemical and biological lab). This lab was a joint venture between France and China, established soon after SARS 2004. Per contract, it could only be used for humanitarian purposes, not to develop "attack capability" purposes.

- In the final phase of design and construction, the Chinese government took over and prohibited France's participation. Later in 2015, France discovered that China cloned the original P4 lab, which is under contract, to have three other P4-like labs. They are all under civilian and military joint ventures and were limited by the original P4 contract.

Then Jay began naming names and talking about viruses in a way I could barely follow. How would I investigate, and what was I to do with the information? (Little did I know that I'd include it in a book with his permission.) I include it here not because I've verified it (other than what I've stated) but because I believe the reader will find it interesting. Of course, time may prove many of these things to be wrong. But if they are true, here is documentation that in early February my anonymous Chinese American source named Jay knew about it long before almost anyone else.

Since I was not able to verify names of the people Jay cited, I am listing only their initials.

- The first person to suspect this new coronavirus was a Jewish retired military officer in early January 2020. He worked in P4 for a few years.

- Later, in mid-January, a group of Indian scientists announced that this virus is a combination of different viruses. The bat virus (SARS) is the mother virus, but it has been genetically altered and mixed with Ebola and the HIV virus. There are traces of segments of RNA genetic code of Ebola and HIV on the new (novel) coronavirus.

- The head of the coronavirus research group of P4 lab, S. Z. published several papers in some scientific journals saying her experiments showed there is an important S protein on human lung cells that serves as a lock mechanism. But on viruses, it can serve as a key to unlock the lung cell and penetrate into lung cells. It is a simple process that only replaces four amino acid molecules to achieve it.

- In the meantime, Canada had already launched an investigation and arrested a Chinese female scientist in Canada. She secretly took coronavirus back to the P4 lab in Wuhan, China, without notifying Canada. Jay said there is a separate investigation and the US FBI had already detained Lieutenant Y. Q., a biology student from Boston. She also secretly brought coronavirus back to the Wuhan P4 lab last summer. She did not disclose who funded her travel.

- There is huge pressure on President Xi to make S. Z. the scapegoat for this pandemic.

At the same time, a well-known Canadian coronavirus scientist, Dr. P., died in Kenya on February 7, only a few days before I received Jay's email. This new coronavirus plague had become a global issue. Jay believed President Trump was right to take the steps he'd taken by early February. Then he went on to express insight into what's really happening with the Communist government and how he sees the Lord's hand in all this. (I'm quoting exactly, other than minor editing of his broken English.) He wrote:

> Unfortunately the Communist Party never spoke the truth. Due to the large number of patients in the early days in Wuhan, only a fraction of patients were able to see doctors. All the hospitals were lacking equipment and other medical resources. Patients were advised to go home to quarantine themselves. So many families all died at home. Per other experts' estimates, the real number of deaths could be one hundred times more than what was published on government websites. [That's because] official numbers were provided only from hospitals.
>
> Why did this happen to China? This disaster is permitted by God to allow the government to make two major mistakes:
>
> 1. Ethical issues. Under government blessing, S. Z. took the lead to do research about coronavirus. She had a joint venture with a US private firm. The goal was to research a mechanism to effectively prevent the spread of coronavirus. It's to save lives. But she found a cheap and quick way to turn coronavirus to be much more virulent and easier to spread and attack human beings. That private firm considered this very unethical and abruptly stopped the funding and withdrew from the joint venture.
>
> 2. Too much blood on "mainland." Throughout seventy years of the reign of the Communist Party, experts estimated there were more than ninety-five million people who died in various revolutions or movements. That is the biggest battleground between freedom and dictatorship.

(China) has too much "hatred." Jesus' "love" is something new. It has never been in people's minds. It's unthinkable to many non-Christian Chinese. God has His time. He has stirred up China for His glory. We estimate there are almost nine hundred million Chinese Christians. They are hidden currently. God is working. Dr. Li Wenliang is a Christian from a house church in Wuhan. [Author note: Wenliang was the whistleblower who died of COVID-19 whom we will discuss more in a moment.] We can see leaked YouTube videos of some Christians in Wuhan passing flyers and free masks and preaching the gospel on the streets. People and government officials accepted in tears. The government doesn't care, or doesn't know how to care, but the children of God do…

Amazing insights. Yet as a Christian journalist, I wasn't sure what to do. Trying to figure how to interpret this, I emailed several doctor friends in the United States to ask if this could "even possibly be true." Two ignored my email. But one doctor of Chinese descent said it sounded like the information her family was getting from their friends in China via the internet.

Two months later this had become much more than a conspiracy theory. US senator Tom Cotton began pressing for an investigation. In an op-ed piece in the *Wall Street Journal*, Cotton wrote, "Beijing has claimed that the virus originated in a Wuhan 'wet market,' where wild animals were sold. But evidence to counter this theory emerged in January. Chinese researchers reported in *The Lancet* on January 24 that the first known cases had no contact with the market, and Chinese state media acknowledged the finding. There's no evidence the market sold bats or pangolins, the animals from which the virus is thought to have jumped to humans. And the bat species that carries it isn't found within one hundred miles of Wuhan."[2]

The *National Review* reported that "Wuhan has two labs where we know bats and humans interacted. One is the Institute of Virology, eight miles from the wet market; the other is the Wuhan Center for Disease Control and Prevention, barely 300 yards from the market."[3]

Senator Cotton further surmised that "this evidence is circumstantial, to be sure, but it all points toward the Wuhan labs," as he concluded in his *Journal* op-ed. "Thanks to the Chinese coverup, we may never have direct, conclusive evidence—intelligence rarely works that way—but Americans justifiably can use common sense to follow the inherent logic of events to their likely conclusion."[4]

I've visited China only once, in the mid-1990s with my friend Dennis Balcombe, an American missionary who has been ministering in Hong Kong for fifty years. I knew he would tell me if he was hearing the same thing and possibly give me advice on how to check it out. (While there I ate cobra the only time in my life, so I knew the Chinese ate exotic animals.)

Through the marvels of the internet, I tracked Dennis down in Africa where he was ministering. We arranged a time to talk via Skype, and I interviewed him for my podcast. He did say he had heard such rumors. However, he gave me what (for Christians who read *Charisma*) was an even greater story: for the church, this has been a blessing in disguise and a great opportunity to pray and spread the gospel. There have been many citywide prayer meetings in which Christians from all groups and different denominations gather to pray and worship, resulting in more unity. Prayer meetings in most churches are much better attended than previously.

Dennis' Revival Christian Church in Hong Kong has a ministry to provide small bottles of disinfectant alcohol, which are in short stock in the stores, free of charge and through this share the gospel with the people in his district. During our interview he told me about a letter he had written to his ministry partners, giving an updated account. After I read it, we got permission to run his letter the next day and embedded my podcast in it, since we covered most of the same topics.

That podcast was listened to by 150,000 people—my biggest audience ever at that time. Obviously there was enormous interest in this topic. Of course, I didn't include the contents of the explosive text I got from Jay, Frank Amedia's Chinese American friend.

But Dennis did give me information of his own. He said this was an exact repeat of the severe acute respiratory syndrome (SARS) epidemic in 2003, which killed 774 worldwide[5] and 299 in Hong Kong.[6] At that time SARS resulted in a huge economic depression to the Hong Kong economy, property and stock market crashes, massive unemployment, yet revival in the church. Due to the fear of possible death resulting from infection by the virus, many came to church and became Christians. It is possible this will be repeated in this COVID-19 pandemic, maybe even on a larger scale.

SARS began in China but spread to Hong Kong through a massive cover-up on the part of the Chinese authorities. History had repeated itself, and one of the headlines in Hong Kong's local newspapers was "Coronavirus: Hundreds in China Sign Petition Calling for Free Speech."[7]

These hundreds were leading intellectuals and academics, many in the medical profession, and they took a great risk to their careers and personal freedom by openly signing a petition calling for additional freedoms and free speech. Their petition to the National People's Congress listed five demands, including one to protect people's rights to freedom of expression.

Sociologist Guo Yuhua of Beijing's Tsinghua University said, "If the warnings were heard much earlier, this outbreak wouldn't have got to the stage of no return."[8] This relates to the death of

Li Wenliang, the ophthalmologist who discovered the virus, who was reprimanded by the police for trying to warn people about the disease outbreak last December. Within a few hours of his death on February 6 there were nearly two million views and fifty-five hundred comments on the Chinese social media Weibo calling for freedom of speech, and many expressed their views that the government owes Dr. Li an apology.[9] The Chinese government quickly censored these comments. But the fact remains that in both SARS and COVID-19, some Chinese authorities put social stability over the welfare and health of the people.

China also has a strict social credit score system, which rates the behaviors of its citizens. As a result of its implementation in recent years, many live in fear of having a reduced score, which severely affects the movement and social status of individuals and subsequently their families as well. Taking this into consideration, it shows us the bravery and boldness it takes for the people to speak out against the government and take a stand against the Communist leadership.

In this case many officials in Wuhan and other parts of Hubei Province who mishandled the crisis have been dismissed from their posts. While nobody can be sure of the future, we can pray that this devastating pandemic will result in more freedoms for the people, including the freedom to share the gospel message.

No one can predict whether this will happen, but we know now that the churches in Wuhan, Hong Kong, and possibly other places rose up to meet the challenge through God's Word and the power of the Holy Spirit. Hong Kong's Revival Christian Church has received testimonies of Christians in Wuhan who were infected with the virus receiving healing through prayer. Even more exciting, reports state that many previously lukewarm believers have renewed their lives and devotion to the Lord.

I knew I couldn't run Jay's report verbatim on Charisma News, but Frank could tell me his perspective. The result was another eye-opening interview, this time with Frank, whose ministry, POTUS Shield, has a close alliance with the Christian community in China. Amedia's sources, who he believes are reliable, can confirm Balcombe's report. Frank had been on my *Strang Report* podcast many times, offering prophetic and spiritual insight into our culture. This time he shed light on what God is doing in the midst of the COVID-19 outbreak.

"We've had reports of Christians being healed of this virus by the power of God and the healing of His Holy Spirit," he said on February 18. "My sources tell me the same thing, whenever there is this kind of a problem—like there was with SARS."

Frank said the coronavirus is the third plague to hit China in the span of this generation. He pointed out that when the people can't rely on their government, they look for help elsewhere—and that's when the church has the opportunity to shine brightly with the gospel, to be the "head and not the tail" (Deut. 28:13).

"We're being told that people are coming in swarms to churches, house churches, that there's gospel and evangelism going out in the streets, person to person, that there's supernatural healing," Frank said.

In our interview Frank also shared some other shocking things about the coronavirus that the media has failed to report. In early February the virus had reportedly killed more than seventeen hundred people and infected over seventy-one thousand. But Frank doesn't believe those numbers are accurate. According to his sources, the numbers of deaths and infections are much higher than media outlets are portraying. In fact, he says the number of deaths is allegedly in the tens of thousands.

"What we're hearing is that while this was being suppressed by the government of China, people were dying in Wuhan, which is the capital of the Hubei Province in the central area of the industrial area of China," Frank said.

"We are told that people were dying before [the existence of the virus] was even admitted. The hospitals didn't know what to do with them. They told them to return home, to stay in their homes, and they were dying," Frank said. "And most of the widespread stories we're getting is that many of them were cremated quickly— some cremated and not even identified for their families, who are still looking for people. [The Chinese authorities] just didn't deal with it appropriately."

Neither was the virus restricted to Wuhan, as some reported, Frank said. Instead, it quickly spread to the four corners of China, and quarantines were put into place. He said this isn't something just his Christian sources told him but also his industrial sources, such as businessmen.

But where did this virus even come from? Again, Frank said it did not come from a marketplace, as was previously thought. Instead, he believes it came from a biosafety level 4 laboratory, Wuhan Institute of Virology, which was located about twenty miles from the marketplace that was originally believed to be the starting point of the virus. This corroborates what news outlets such as the *National Review* have reported (though that report estimates the lab to be just eight miles from the now-infamous Wuhan wet market).

"These are high-level biosafety laboratories," Amedia said. "This laboratory was established in a joint venture [with] the French government starting back in 2004 as a response to the SARS [virus] so that the Chinese government would have a research lab for humanitarian purposes and to develop vaccines."

But the French backed out of that joint venture a few years ago when they found out the Chinese had replicated this laboratory,

Frank said, using it for privately owned businesses. As noted previously, Sen. Tom Cotton of Arkansas spoke out about this, though some labeled his words a conspiracy theory. According to Frank, the Chinese ambassador to the United States, Cui Tiankai, did not deny that it could have come out of this lab, which surprised the White House.

Will the public ever know what really caused the coronavirus? Will the full truth ever come out? We may never know, but God can still continue to move powerfully through this horrible situation. That's why Christians around the world must keep praying for this virus to be contained and eliminated. But we must also pray that in response to this frightening pandemic, people will keep flocking to Jesus Christ and create a revival not only in China but throughout the world, which I deal with in a later chapter.

Chapter 4

TRUMP, THE ECONOMY, AND COVID-19

IN MARCH, JUST as the country was shutting down due to COVID-19, the overwhelming surge in unemployment filings came as a hard pill to swallow for our nation. With companies of all sizes hit by the fallout from COVID-19, many Americans began scrambling for their next paychecks. As with all historical economic slumps, minorities and young workers experienced a significant impact.

A recent report by Moody's Analytics chief economist Mark Zandi identified the hardest-hit industries. These include "leisure and hospitality (16.9 million people), transportation (5.7 million), employment services (3.7 million), mining (662,000), and travel arrangements (222,000)." Because 17.6 percent of Hispanic workers and 16.8 percent of African American workers are in these areas, compared with 12.5 percent of non-Hispanic white workers, experts anticipate that Hispanic and black Americans will lose jobs at higher rates during a coronavirus-led recession than other groups.[1]

Up to this point, the Trump administration has been able to maintain the lowest black American unemployment rates in history. In February the Department of Labor reported a rate of 5.8 percent.[2]

Will the great strides President Trump has made with the black community be lost because of this current situation? In *God, Trump, and the 2020 Election* I discuss why the president could lose in 2020, but a virus was never in the mix—until now.

The global spread of the coronavirus is heightening Americans' anxiety, which is reflected in the volatile stock market. With so much uncertainty surrounding both the economy and the 2020 election, many people are asking whether the pandemic is a "black swan" event. Just look at the headlines. *Politico* reported, "Trump Faces 'Black Swan' Threat to the Economy and Reelection."[3] And then there was this opinion piece in the *New Yorker* titled, "As the Coronavirus Spreads, Stocks Fall Again and the White House Frets About a Black Swan."[4]

It almost seems as though this is exactly what those who oppose our president wanted to happen. In fact, political commentator Bill Maher said on his HBO show *Real Time* in 2018 that he was "hoping" the economy would crash to "get rid of Trump."[5]

The phrase *black swan* gained popularity during the Great Recession, largely thanks to essayist and investor Nassim Nicholas Taleb's best-selling book *The Black Swan*. The 2007 book released just months before the banking and housing crises that brought on the devastating economic downturn and gave its readers a new way of thinking about potential risks that were both extremely damaging and extremely rare.

According to Taleb, a black swan is, first, "an *outlier*, as it lies outside the realm of regular expectations, because nothing in the past can convincingly point to its possibility. Second, it carries an extreme impact (unlike the bird). Third, in spite of its outlier status, human nature makes us concoct explanations for its occurrence *after* the fact, making it explainable and predictable."[6]

With the Left hardly veiling its hopes that the pandemic will thwart Trump's reelection, some have gone so far as to think there could be a nefarious agenda in this whole situation. Others say the Democrats and those who oppose the president are simply maximizing this crisis for political gain. As the saying goes, "Never let a good crisis go to waste."

The coronavirus came just as the black community was beginning to look at Trump differently due to his success in bringing benefits their way that the Democrats have never delivered.

Most black voters continue to follow Democratic Party lines—although something strange happened in the 2016 election. Though only 8 percent of black Americans voted for Trump, many stayed home rather than voting for Clinton. The *New York Times* found that 4.4 million Obama voters stayed home on Election Day, and more than a third of those no-shows—1.6 million—were black Americans.[7]

Before the COVID-19 outbreak, Trump's 2020 campaign manager, Brad Parscale, said Trump could quadruple the 2016 black voter turnout in 2020, according to a 2019 article on RealClear Politics by Philip Wegmann titled "Trump Bets on More Black Support in 2020. (He Might Need It.)." Wegmann quoted a Daily Beast article in which longtime GOP strategist Ed Rollins said, "Democrats can't win unless they get Obama levels of black voter turnout. Unless they can get back to those levels, it makes it awful hard for them to win the White House."[8]

Despite Trump's efforts to reach out to the black community and create economic opportunities for all Americans, an NBC News/*Wall Street Journal* poll from February 2020 found that a mere 14 percent of black voters have a positive view of the president.[9] But the Trump campaign sees an opportunity to make the case that Democrats have taken black voters for granted.

Of course, this was before we knew how serious the coronavirus is or that in three weeks of quarantine the gains in the economy would be wiped out. And of course, the coronavirus won't last forever. The president is bullish on how the economy will come roaring back. During this shutdown dealing with one of the worst pandemics of our lifetime, it seems the election has been moved to the back burner. The presumed Democratic nominee, Joe Biden, was quarantined in his basement, while the president, who is the dynamic leader Biden has never been, is showing leadership at a whole new level.

I admire the way Trump has delegated much of the decision-making to the states, as it should be, and has looked to the private sector for answers instead of assuming everything should be done through Washington. He has removed regulations, marshaled the military to use ships as hospitals, and shown the leadership necessary to bring us through this crisis.

Though some Democrats have accused the president of grabbing power, he has done just the opposite: He chose to let our federal system work and to delegate much of the decision-making to the fifty governors rather than direct everything from a bigger and bigger executive branch bureaucracy in Washington. In addition, he has used his negotiating skills to unite the government and public sector and unleash the creativity of the American people to come up with solutions.

Trump's daily pressers have communicated directly to the American people to teach, explain, or persuade, but mostly to reassure them that the unprecedented pandemic is being handled as well as it can be. Not surprisingly the Left is trying to paint a different picture and blame him for COVID-19, with some Democrats even calling it the "Trump Virus."[10]

I've shifted my focus to reporting on the pandemic, and my *Strang Report* podcast numbers have gone through the roof. People can't seem to get enough information, especially from a source they can trust for the spiritual dimension.

We Christians believe this pandemic did not catch God by

surprise. We believe He hears and answers prayer. I personally believe He gave us our president for such a time as this. We also know the Bible is true: "We know that all things work together for good to those who love God, to those who are called according to His purpose" (Rom. 8:28).

In the black community the so-called "black church" is a very strong influence—more so than most denominations are in the majority community. I've spent my career covering the black Christian community in *Charisma* because it makes up a sizable percentage of the Pentecostal movement. Indeed, Pentecostalism grew out of the 1906 Azusa Street Revival, which was led by a black preacher named William Seymour.

I believe these black Christians—who usually support the Democratic Party—are beginning to look at Trump differently.

However, I've had black preacher friends say they overlook the bad policies of the Democrats (such as those regarding abortion and gay marriage) in the same way white Christians overlook the many faults of the Republican Party just because the Republicans back certain "Christian" causes.

In *God, Trump, and the 2020 Election* I tell the story of Candace Owens, a well-known conservative activist who began the movement called Blexit in 2018. The campaign, which promotes the exit of black Americans from the Democratic Party, is now a nationwide movement. Owens and others are working to stop the narrative that Trump is racist, one she says is propagated by the left-leaning media.

Owens has defended Trump against accusations of racism from black leftists, saying, "Black support for Donald Trump has doubled since this time last year. You guys can try to pretend that he is pushing in a racist era in this country when in fact we know the Democrats are the racists. [They] have always been the racists; the parties never switched, and you should know this.... You know the people under the hood of the KKK were Democrats, and the parties never switched. And it's a shame you should defend…our community being attacked because we support Donald Trump because we understand that we have better economic opportunities under him than we ever had [with] Obama….I'm really done with this. I'm done with this racist narrative."[11]

But calling Trump a racist is nothing new. Democrats have been using the epithet to label any Republican they don't like. The article on RealClear Politics about black voter support for Trump said, "This condemnation…has become something of a litmus test in the Democratic primary, with candidates lining up one after the other to decry the current occupant of the Oval Office."[12]

Yet the perception remains in the black community and media that if you're black, you must be a Democrat. Not only that, but the media also vilifies every black person who is Republican or supports President Trump. In my book *Trump Aftershock*, I devoted an entire chapter to "Billionaire Radicals," documenting how many believe Democrat super-donor George Soros (and others) helped fuel the fire of division. He often invests heavily in the organization and logistics of what are meant to appear as grassroots efforts that subsequently materialize as protests, rallies, and marches.

These are not organic in nature but are methodically coordinated operations intended to help stoke the flames of racial and ideological division. The liberal media often highlights these stories and then further amplifies them to increase their effectiveness. Soros seems to be a firm believer in the extreme-Left doctrine found in Saul Alinsky's book *Rules for Radicals*.

The good news is most black Americans who back the president are not turning their backs on him, because they see what he's accomplishing and what he's doing for the black community—even with all the new economic problems associated with the COVID-19 pandemic. The president wants to reach the black community, and I hope the people will begin to see that—especially during the time of rebuilding. Black America needs a strong leader such as Donald Trump as we move to recovery, just as all of America does. I make this point clear in *God, Trump, and the 2020 Election* because the issues of leadership and the direction of our nation were important before the outbreak of COVID-19, and they're even more important now.

Chapter 5

DAMNED IF HE DOES,
DAMNED IF HE DOESN'T

I F DONALD TRUMP were to find the cure for cancer tomorrow, his critics would accuse him of putting doctors out of work. They would use the full media apparatus to try and discredit his announcement and label him and his groundbreaking discovery fraudulent. They would tell people not to get the treatment, go on a full media blitz about why it is so "dangerous," and do their best to put fear into the hearts and minds of innocent Americans who truly need the help.

We know this by watching many examples and because if the president were to get positive coverage of the very successful and monumental achievements of his first term in office, he most likely would have the highest approval ratings of any president in recent history. Just look at the crowds he was able to attract when he was having his rallies. Even with the media spin, many Americans are waking up to the extreme bias.

Never have we seen the mainstream corporate media so united against anyone in our lifetime—especially a president. I remember in the anti–Vietnam War era the intense hatred toward Richard Nixon. Since then former presidents Reagan, George H. W. Bush, Clinton, and George W. Bush have had their challenges with the press, but nothing like this.

Why the hatred of Trump? It must be that Trump is onto something; otherwise why would the six corporations that control 90 percent of the mainstream media (including Fox News) be so united in their attempt to take this man down? Their efforts are tireless—even relentless. They attempt to wear down those who support the president. He's had to battle to get hydroxychloroquine into the hands of doctors on the front lines, even though it has proved quite effective. (More on this later.) That once again proves this point.

In the COVID-19 pandemic, we have seen that same media apparatus continue with its vicious and daily attacks. Sometimes I get frustrated watching the outright lack of respect some in the White House press corps have for the president as he gives his coronavirus briefings along with the task force. Even if they don't like him, they could still show honor and respect for his office; instead, there is a blatant disregard. It's quite honestly embarrassing to watch. What must other countries think of our press? What example are these reporters showing our young people? To me it's a spirit of rebellion.

Think about what Trump has had to endure. The same week Democrats were trying to impeach him, he banned travel from China to the United States when it became clear that the pneumonia-like virus that, as late as January 14, the Chinese said could not be transmitted from human to human was getting out of hand. In typical nature the Left continued with its usual accusations, screaming that he was "xenophobic."[1] Interestingly, House Speaker Nancy Pelosi actually deleted a tweet in which she encouraged people to "go to Chinatown," and she both mocked and attacked the president in her usual tirades.

The truth is, the president has shown tremendous leadership in all of this. His quick action in implementing the travel ban from China January 31 and then from Europe in mid-March probably saved hundreds of thousands of lives. As bad as the coronavirus is and as many lives as it has taken, it would have been far worse had he not acted so quickly.

The good news for Trump is that people don't forget easily,

and there is an army of social media influencers who show the Democrats' own words over and over again to those who may have forgotten. There is nothing more convincing than simply replaying leftists' own interviews and clips on social media so people can see just how hypocritical they are. That's because in the facts war, Trump wins hands down. That is one reason the socialist and Deep State opposition are so afraid.

But regardless, the Left has changed its narrative once again and is now trashing Trump in this way—saying he did too little too late. My own theory is that those on the left want to drag this out as long as they can, hoping the economy is so bad that something weird may happen and their weak and ill-equipped candidate Joe Biden may slip into office on Election Day. They have such a deep lust for power that they'd rather have the economy stop if it meant they could win. Just read what liberal political commentator Bill Mayer said: "I feel like the bottom has to fall out at some point. And by the way, I'm hoping for it....One way you get rid of Trump is a crashing economy. So, please, bring on the recession."[2] Can you get any more anti-American than that? Why would anyone who supposedly loves our country wish this upon us?

The truth is, the Left is especially fearful because of the great gains Trump already brought to our economy. Even secular observers such as Dr. Michael Busler, professor of finance at Stockton University, agreed in a Townhall op-ed that President Trump's achievements are truly remarkable.

Busler observes that when Trump was elected in 2016, the nation was in a ten-year economic slump averaging only 2 percent growth—the first time in history the economy did not hit 3 percent growth in a decade. That led to poor employment prospects and stagnant wages, which led to resentment, causing some citizens to embrace socialism and reject capitalism. "The country was headed in an un-American direction," Busler wrote.[3]

Not only was the economy weak, but so was our soft foreign policy, with bad actors in Russia, China, the Middle East, and North Korea. At the same time, many Americans began to place security above freedom, wanting the government to provide a basic income or housing and pay for their health care or higher education. There was also resentment in the heartland and the belief that the country was headed in the wrong direction. Busler notes: "So Donald Trump came along. He was a very, very successful business-person and TV personality. Although elected president, he was not a politician. But Trump's message was welcomed by Americans. He told people to look in the mirror. He asked them to see where they were and what they had."

Trump then asked, "What do you have to lose?"

His "Make America Great Again" mantra emphasized a return to prosperity. His vision was always clear. His policies made the economy boom, and he also rebuilt the military and adopted a foreign policy of "peace through strength."

Busler concluded: "History will note that Donald Trump was remarkable. In spite of more than 90 percent of media coverage of him being negative, in spite of every Democrat consistently opposing anything he wants to do, and in spite of some members of his own party being against him, he has managed to change the direction of the country."[4]

So what did Trump really do regarding the coronavirus? Cleta Mitchell, a partner in the Washington, DC, office of Foley and Lardner, writing for *The Federalist*, gives insight into the timetable of what Trump did and when. Of course, this is an evolving story, and only historians can really evaluate what happened. Trump will be judged on his handling of this unparalleled pandemic.

Nevertheless, the Democrats immediately began talking about a new investigation into how the president "mishandled" the coronavirus response as another way to attack him in the upcoming months to try to affect the outcome of the presidential election. We can almost be assured this will be part of the strategy as the next few months play out.

"The leftist national media incessantly reports that the spread of the coronavirus is, well, President Trump's fault. House Speaker Nancy Pelosi, always good for the most incendiary and least helpful comments in any difficult situation, said on Sunday, 'the president—his denial at the beginning was deadly,'" Mitchell wrote in *The Federalist* on March 31.[5] Joe Biden did the same in a feeble effort to make his campaign relevant.

Here is a key fact: In the beginning China lied. People died. The World Health Organization (WHO) and Centers for Disease Control and Prevention (CDC) also got it wrong. Although the first case of the coronavirus was reported in Wuhan, China, in early December 2019, through January 2020 the Chinese authorities continued to downplay the potential for the disease to spread.

The WHO reinforced China's falsehoods, saying on January 14 that "preliminary investigations conducted by the Chinese authorities have found no clear evidence of human-to-human transmission of the novel coronavirus (2019-nCoV) identified in Wuhan, China." This was five to six weeks after the opposite was confirmed to be the case in Wuhan.

Biden's supposed chronicle of Trump administration failures derides the president's statement on January 22, saying, "We have it totally under control, it is one person, coming in from China."[6] What was actually happening in the United States on January 22? It was one person coming in from China. And the US CDC had yet to confirm the nation's first person-to-person transmission of the coronavirus—that did not happen until January 30, 2020.[7] Democrats and the mainstream media have a ubiquitous influence on each other. In other words, it certainly appears they get the same talking points and work in tandem to achieve an agenda.

"If Pelosi believes the president should have done something at the beginning, when exactly does she think was the 'beginning'? Was it during the impeachment proceedings that Pelosi instigated? Should Pelosi bear some responsibility for what she perceives as the president's failure to focus on the coronavirus back in January?" Cleta Mitchell wrote.[8] Isn't that exactly when Pelosi was saying it was "just like a flu" and accusing the president of being a "xenophobe"?

I believe closing travel from China on January 31 was probably the single most important action the president took during the early stages of the pandemic. And when he reminds us of that fact in nearly every daily White House briefing, he doesn't also say, as Mitchell points out, that at the time "the CDC was assuring us the risk to America was low, the WHO was covering for China, Democrats were trying to impeach the president, and Biden was attacking the decision as 'xenophobic.'"

Mitchell concludes: "It is impossible to overestimate the number of American lives saved by that momentous decision by President Trump on January 31. And no media or Pelosi false narratives or phony Biden campaign ad can change the truth about the real chronology of the coronavirus."[9]

It just kept going. "Easter Sunday was not all that peaceful for President Trump because he found himself correcting several false headlines and 'fake news' on Twitter," Cortney O'Brien wrote on Townhall.[10]

So much disinformation comes out that the president must personally set the record straight. For example, on Easter he tweeted that "if the Fake News Opposition Party is pushing, with all their might, the fact that President Trump 'ignored early warnings about the threat,' then why did Media & Dems viciously criticize me when I instituted a Travel Ban on China? They said 'early & not necessary.' Corrupt Media!"[11]

He later did a callout to One America News (who he thinks gets it right): "Sorry Fake News, it's all on tape. I banned China long before people spoke up. Thank you @OANN."[12]

Sometimes I find the follow-up tweets as enlightening as the president's, such as this one from Republican congressional candidate DeAnna Lorraine, who tweeted: "Fauci is now saying that had Trump listened to the medical experts earlier he could've saved more lives." Dr. Fauci was telling people on February 29 that there was nothing to worry about and the coronavirus posed no threat to the US public at large. Again, they think we have no memory.[13]

The fact is, Cortney O'Brien pointed out in her Townhall op-ed that Dr. Fauci has praised the president's travel ban as a great help in the fight against COVID-19 in the United States. Former vice president Joe Biden, who originally called the travel ban "xeno-phobic," finally gave his belated approval.[14] (It's important to add here that Dr. Fauci has some very interesting ties to Big Pharma. He sits on the leadership council at the Gates Foundation. I should mention many spiritually discerning Christians have said they have a "check in their spirit" with regard to this man and his intentions.)

O'Brien wrote: "Trump's Twitter campaign to correct disinfor-mation has been supplemented by his daily White House corona-virus task force briefings, where he's sparred with reporters who are clearly less interested in getting important information to the public, and more interested in trying to pin the entire outbreak on the pres-ident or accuse him of downplaying the health crisis. But for each partisan question, Trump always has an answer."[15]

Easter, however, wasn't spent just criticizing the media. Instead, the president "gave a positive Easter message, and told the American people that we can and will defeat the 'invisible enemy,'" O'Brien concluded.[16]

Regardless of the relentless attacks, this president is like a bulldozer. He may be the only person I can think of who could have taken such a daily beating and yet continue to win, pushing back against the nefarious agenda and those who seek to destroy him and our country. This is most likely why God chose him to lead us through this very significant time in history as we battle for the very future of our country.

This is exactly why I fight as well. We have to keep pressing ahead, knowing that the God of heaven and earth is with us every step of the way. This most certainly is a spiritual battle, which is why we must dig into these concerns a little more in the next chapter. We, as believers, need to truly be watchmen on the wall and understand the true battle at hand.

Chapter 6

ALARMING ANTI-CHRISTIAN TRENDS

A T THE BEGINNING of 2020 none of us expected this pandemic. And few expected that battling the outbreak would create governmental powers in which America would begin to look like a police state. As new restrictions on gatherings were lowered to fifty and then again to fewer than ten people, it quickly became apparent that this pandemic would be a game changer. Going to sporting events, movies, theatrical events, concerts, and church meetings was suddenly forbidden.

New York Mayor Bill de Blasio threatened to close churches and synagogues "permanently" if they refused to shut down during the pandemic.[1] And Virginia governor Ralph Northam declared that church gatherings of ten or more could result in a $2,500 fine and up to a year in jail.[2]

Northam's approach is much like the tactic taken in France. My friend Ken Timmerman from Florida was stuck in France on Easter and gave me an eyewitness account of the total lockdown. He said French President Emmanuel Macron issued an order that if you attended church once, you would receive a $150 fine. Twice, and the fine became $1,500. The third time, you would go to jail for six months. Many started to point out how grocery stores and other businesses that were deemed "essential" sometimes had hundreds of people in the store at one time. So why were churches so quickly deemed "nonessential"? And why was the public so quick to accept this? It rapidly escalated to a hot debate in the Christian community.

As I touched on in the introduction, Pastor Rodney Howard-Browne, a longtime friend of mine, was arrested and booked into a local jail on Monday, March 30, after holding Sunday worship services at The River at Tampa Bay, the church he leads. Howard-Browne was charged with unlawful assembly and violating the county's stay-at-home order. He was later released on bail.

Originally coming to the United States as a missionary from South Africa, Pastor Rodney has been holding services where God's presence has been moving in power for many years. His intention was to allow the Holy Spirit to move and heal the sick as they would come for prayer. After all, that is what the Bible says to do as believers.

The media loved this story—"crazy Pentecostal pastor endangers the health of his church members by recklessly disregarding governmental edicts for no 'nonessential' gatherings over ten people." But the case brought up some interesting legal issues.

Whether churches are "essential" in the midst of this coronavirus crisis is a critical question that must take into consideration many factors. The related question, whether churches should open or close, must be considered in the context of each church and community.

Mat Staver, founder of Liberty Counsel, came to Howard-Browne's defense, and the results were amazing. The county dropped the case because Staver sued for violation of the church's constitutional rights to freedom of religion and freedom of assembly. On Charisma News we published an op-ed by Liberty Counsel stating its position in the case.

To navigate the media storm in wisdom and present the actual situation to the public after a heated debate had erupted, Liberty Counsel gave an articulate explanation, stating: "It is important to present the real facts surrounding the recent arrest of the pastor of The River at Tampa Bay. Many of the statements made by

Hillsborough County Sheriff Chad Chronister are false. His statements have put both the pastor and the church in danger."

The rest of the statement read as follows:[3]

On Thursday, March 26, Sheriff Chronister told the pastor and other staff members by speakerphone that the church could meet on Sunday, March 29, and that he had no intention of shutting it down, and no intention of arresting anyone. He gave these assurances after he was informed of all the precautions the church proposed to undertake, including encouraging seniors or people with predisposed health conditions to stay home, limiting attendance by enforcing a 6-foot separation, requiring each person to use hand sanitizers upon entry and installing over $100,000 of high-grade hospital air purifiers. A deputy sheriff also toured the church to inspect the premises the same day.

The meeting with Sheriff Chronister and his deputy on March 26 was called to discuss the draft Hillsborough County order presented by the council the same day. That order was then passed on Friday, March 27, and went into effect at 10 p.m. This was the first and only enforceable order passed by the county. Based on this order and the fact that the church went above and beyond the health guidance, the sheriff gave the green light for the church to meet. On Saturday, March 28, the church was thoroughly sanitized. On Sunday, March 29, the church met. Then on Monday, the same sheriff who gave the green light to meet a few days earlier held a press conference announcing the pastor's arrest, during which Sheriff Chronister made many false statements.

Following the pastor's arrest, on Wednesday, April 1, Florida Governor Ron DeSantis issued Executive Order 2020-91, stating: "Attending religious services conducted in churches, synagogues and houses of worship" is an "essential activity."

The same day, Executive Order 2020-92 required that his order supersede any contrary local government order respecting essential services and activities. The Hillsborough County order restricting churches was therefore overruled.

To answer the question of whether churches are essential and whether the doors should be opened or closed requires a review of each case. There are an estimated 500,000 or more Protestant, Catholic, and Orthodox churches in America. These range from small to large, and each church has a different community of service or people who attend. The people who attend and the community they serve run the gamut from old to young, upper class, middle class, poor, urban, rural, inner city, country and include a wide variety of ethnic, racial, and language diversity.

Based on the demographics of the people who attend and the capability to broadcast online, some churches are better off if they close through this time. However, some churches provide essential ministries, besides music and the pastor preaching from the pulpit, which cannot be carried out online.

The River Church feeds 900 people each week by providing free food from its farmer's market located inside the church lobby. The church grows its own food and farms tilapia to give to the community. When the doors of this church close, people starve, including children.

Many people are experiencing increased stress. Many have lost their jobs and do not know where they will get the next meal. Many people suffer from mental, emotional and physical pain. Those with intractable physical pain are not able to get relief from their chiropractor, physical therapist or pain management specialist. Experiencing pain 24/7 often leads to depression and even suicide.

Battered women are locked in their homes with the abuser. Children are out of school and are restricted in some places from going to the parks or beaches. Without work, the extra stress can become overwhelming.

Some churches provide counseling. Some provide food, clothes and money to those in need.

The River Church serves a large community that has no access to the internet. Even some people who have access to the internet lack the bandwidth to watch a service online.

To answer the question of whether a church is essential and whether it should open or close its doors, people need to look beyond their own circumstances to see the mounting needs and hurting people who are less fortunate and who need the ministry of the local church.

No shepherd of the flock wants to do anything that would endanger the community. But the question is, should we allow some discretion to follow health guidelines while determining what can and cannot be provided online? Or do we want to give this unfettered authority to a single government official?

Perhaps it is important to reconsider what is essential about the church. Some are far more essential than others. A blanket answer to the question is too simple and serves a grave injustice to many.

Maybe there should be more discretion given to the shepherds of the church to determine whether the church should meet, and if so, how best may the church protect those who attend and serve the needs of the community. This is a much better approach than a one-size-fits-all template that labels churches as "non-essential."

The above says nothing about the constitutional rights of churches under the First Amendment and the statutory rights under the Religious Land Use and Institutionalized Persons Act. These rights do not evaporate in a time of crisis.

Are we willing to allow one person, whether state or local, to have the unchecked discretion to write a church into or out of existence by one word—the word "essential"? Such authority is extraordinary and runs counter to American history.

The last question is one for the church: "Is the ministry of the church so essential that the community groans in its absence?" If any church is not that essential, then maybe that church needs to ponder what changes should be made in order to be the essential lighthouse and place of refuge that God desires.

The issue is facing pastors across the country. In Kentucky, Louisville Mayor Greg Fischer issued a ban the week before Easter preventing churches from holding even drive-in services. He said with Louisville's urban population, "it's not really practical or safe to allow drive-up services." Fischer said such a move would result in "hundreds of thousands of people driving around" on Sundays instead of remaining home to slow the spread of the novel coronavirus.[4]

On Fire Christian Center sued the mayor, and on the Saturday before Easter, Federal District Judge Justin Walker issued a temporary injunction allowing the church to proceed with its drive-in services. The order was abundantly clear: "The court enjoins Louisville from enforcing; attempting to enforce; threatening to enforce; or otherwise requiring compliance with any prohibition on drive-in church services at On Fire."[5]

The judge began his opinion by acknowledging his shock that the injunction was even necessary.

On Holy Thursday, an American mayor criminalized the communal celebration of Easter.

That sentence is one that this Court never expected to see outside the pages of a dystopian novel, or perhaps the pages of *The Onion*. But two days ago, citing the need for social distancing during the current pandemic, Louisville's Mayor Greg

Fischer ordered Christians not to attend Sunday services, even if they remained *in their cars* to worship—and even though it's *Easter*.

The Mayor's decision is stunning.

And it is, "beyond all reason," unconstitutional.

The opinion gave a brief history of the Plymouth Colony, pointing out that the Pilgrims found in the New World "what they wanted most, what they needed most: the liberty to worship God according to their conscience."

The Pilgrims were heirs to a long line of persecuted Christians, including some punished with prison or worse for the crime of celebrating Easter—and an even longer line of persecuted peoples of more ancient faiths. And although their notions of tolerance left more than a little to be desired, the Pilgrims understood at least this much: *No* place, not even the unknown, is worse than any place whose state forbids the exercise of your sincerely held religious beliefs.

He said the Pilgrims' history of fleeing religious persecution "was just one of the many 'historical instances of religious persecution and intolerance that gave concern to those who drafted the Free Exercise Clause' of our Constitution's First Amendment."[6]

Judge Walker also cited comments from the Louisville mayor and Kentucky governor warning that police had been ordered to collect license plates of those participating in drive-in church services and that the health department would follow up with them to ensure they were quarantined for fourteen days.

The authorities, he said, were applying a double standard that violated the Free Exercise Clause.

Louisville has targeted religious worship by prohibiting drive-in church services, while not prohibiting a multitude of other non-religious drive-ins and drive-throughs—including, for example, drive-through liquor stores. Moreover, Louisville has not prohibited parking in parking lots more broadly—including, again, the parking lots of liquor stores. When Louisville prohibits religious activity while permitting non-religious activities, its choice "must undergo the most rigorous of scrutiny."

Mayor Fischer had been encouraging residents to participate in online services, but Judge Walker said that does not satisfy the burden of the Free Exercise Clause.

> Louisville might suggest that On Fire members could participate in an online service and thus satisfy their longing for communal celebration. But some members may not have access to online resources. And even if they all did, the Free Exercise Clause protects their right to worship as their conscience commands them. It is not the role of a court to tell religious believers what is and isn't important to their religion, so long as their belief in the religious importance is sincere. The Free Exercise clause protects sincerely held religious beliefs that are at times not "acceptable, logical, consistent, or comprehensible to others."

The court even noted that "the Greek word translated 'church' in our English versions of the Christian Scriptures is the word *ekklesia*, which literally means 'assembly.'"

According to the court documents, the church committed to practicing the CDC's social distancing guidelines, saying "cars will park six feet apart and all congregants will remain in their cars with windows no more than half open for the entirety of the service." Only the pastor and a videographer would stand outside, and the pastor would preach over a loudspeaker.

Mayor Fischer later reversed his ban after On Fire congregants were met with nails at the entrances and exits to the church parking lot.[7]

Although the church was represented by First Liberty Institute, WilmerHale, and Swansburg & Smith, Liberty Counsel had been monitoring the case. Mat Staver said:

> The decision by Judge Justin Walker underscores the fact that the First Amendment does not evaporate even during a crisis. Many of the restrictions across the country on churches and houses of worship are unconstitutional because they prohibit religious gatherings while allowing a multitude of non-religious gatherings. Mass gatherings are permitted in liquor stores, Home Depot, and a multitude of retail stores. When smaller and less frequent gatherings are prohibited in church parking lots or with social distancing inside the church while allowed in a myriad of secular commercial locations, the First Amendment demands rigorous scrutiny of the government's choices.[8]

Meanwhile, a California pastor resigned from his position on the city council a day before he challenged state social distancing guidelines by holding an in-person Palm Sunday Communion service.

Rob McCoy, senior pastor of Godspeak Calvary Chapel in Newbury Park, had been on the Thousand Oaks City Council since 2015 and had previously served as mayor of the city for a year. Although his church had been livestreaming its services, he said he felt a deep conviction to offer in-person Communion to his congregation, which would be available after the online service from 1:00 to 3:00 p.m. McCoy knew the move would put him in violation of the social distancing guidelines that prohibit gatherings of ten or more people, which is why he stepped down from his post. But he said it is a mistake to classify churches as nonessential.

"Palm Sunday and Resurrection Sunday are critical," McCoy said in a video announcing the Palm Sunday Communion. "[We are being] paralyzed and considered nonessential, though we would have liquor stores considered essential, cannabis distribution considered essential....Across the country, abortions are considered essential. Is the church going to sit back and say, 'Well, we'll be relegated to nonessential,' though we feed people, and [physical food] is essential? We are essential—essential for the simple fact that God called us to this."

The church mapped out strict social-distancing guidelines for the service. Only ten people would be allowed in the building at a time, and the congregants were directed through the service with arrows positioned six feet apart. Church members were reminded to sit six feet apart when inside the building, and they were cautioned to keep a proper distance from other participants when outside.

"We want to honor Caesar," McCoy said in the video. "We want to render unto Caesar what is Caesar's. We want to respect social distancing. We want to respect everything that is expected of us. But we still want to have access to what is a sacrament in the Protestant church and the Catholic Church as well."

The church urged those who were sick to stay home and those who were able to wear masks. Those who didn't feel comfortable leaving their cars could have someone deliver the Communion elements to them. The church even offered to deliver Communion to members at home.

"We find Communion; we find community—common unity— in this sacrament," McCoy said. "It's critical to the body of Christ....To not allow us to have access to Communion is not proper. To consider it nonessential is not acceptable."[9]

McCoy, of course, was attacked for his decision to hold the service. On the day of the Communion service, protestors lined up in their cars and honked their horns at participants, the *Los Angeles*

Times reported. The newspaper added that Thousand Oaks police officers were to be on hand to ensure church members kept proper distance.[10]

It may have felt like a strange turn of events for McCoy. He had been applauded for his leadership after the mass shooting at the Borderline Bar and Grill that left twelve dead[11] and the Woolsey fire that destroyed nearly one hundred thousand acres and sixteen hundred structures.[12] Both tragedies took place in November 2018, and the following month McCoy became mayor of Thousand Oaks and remained in that position for a year. When his tenure ended, he was hailed as "the right mayor at the right time" and "the right mayor to heal" and unite his city.[13]

In a statement responding to McCoy's resignation, Thousand Oaks Mayor Al Adam commended McCoy's leadership, calling him "a voice of strength and healing" as the city recovered from the Borderline and Woolsey tragedies. "I appreciate his contributions and wish him and his family well," Adam said. "While these circumstances are unfortunate, the remaining members of the Council and I are very much focused on moving forward."[14]

Thankfully Christian law firms are defending freedom against these anti-God trends in the culture that manifested themselves during this time of crisis. The double standard has been obvious.

As the country went into lockdown mode, America's pro-life leaders voiced alarm that churches were being forced to close down, while in most states abortion clinics were allowed to stay open.

"How dare they jail pastors and close the doors of the church while the abortion industry remains open to spread the virus and put our lives at risk?" said Janet Porter, president and founder of Faith2Action (f2a.org) and the author of the original pro-life Heartbeat Bill.[15]

"While free speech and freedom of religion are being banned,

Planned Parenthood continues to get away with murder," said Mark Harrington, president of Created Equal, a pro-life group. "The cure is now worse than the disease."[16]

"In a pandemic, a double standard is deadly," Porter said. "Either there is a threat or there isn't. We must either close the doors of the abortion business or open the doors of the church."

"By definition, the surgeries abortion centers perform are *elective*—that's why they call it 'choice,'" said Harrington.[17]

To classify abortion as "essential medical care" during the novel coronavirus crisis is "preposterous," said Mark Crutcher, founder and president of Life Dynamics, a Texas-based pro-life organization. "Abortion providers don't care that there's a pandemic. All they care about is killing babies. There can be no sacred cows in a pandemic. It is indefensible."[18]

In late March, when states were developing their coronavirus responses, the governors of Ohio, Texas, and Mississippi vowed to halt abortions during the COVID-19 pandemic.

Ohio was the first to stop abortion clinics from performing "non-essential and elective surgical abortions." On March 21, Ohio Attorney General Dave Yost sent a letter to clinics ordering them to stop abortions in order to preserve personal protective equipment such as face masks, reported NBC4 in Columbus.[19]

Then Texas Republican governor Greg Abbott issued an executive order to halt elective procedures so as to expand hospital bed capacity. That included any abortions not deemed medically necessary. "No one is exempt from the governor's executive order on medically unnecessary surgeries and procedures, including abortion providers," Attorney General Ken Paxton said. "Those who violate the governor's order will be met with the full force of the law."[20]

Republican Mississippi governor Tate Reeves followed suit, saying he would take action against abortion clinics if they continued offering abortions during the COVID-19 outbreak, *The Hill* reported. He too said abortions should count as elective procedures.[21]

In a statement issued March 26, Dr. James Dobson, host of Family Talk radio and founder of Focus on the Family, praised the governors of Texas and Ohio for their bold decisions and said other governors across the nation should follow their example.

> Our nation and our world are in the midst of a pandemic that is claiming thousands of lives, and the US is taking drastic measures to protect people during this unprecedented time.
>
> So why are abortionists seeking to operate business as usual?
>
> Abortion is neither health care nor essential. It is the ultimate selfish act, the taking of lives in the name of "choice." Abortion is not life-protecting—it ends the life of an unborn child, and irreversibly changes the lives of so many others.
>
> Thankfully, some governors are taking action and issuing executive orders to halt "elective surgeries"—this should most certainly include abortion procedures. Texas Governor Greg Abbott and Ohio Governor Mike DeWine are two who have acted decisively and boldly. They have my deepest thanks!
>
> But where are the other 48? As my friend Janet Porter, president of Faith2Action, says, "There can be no 'sacred cows' in a pandemic." Let's remind every governor of this reality, and demand that they order Planned Parenthood and its ilk to put up the "closed" sign. During this unparalleled health crisis, we need to be about saving lives and not carrying out this blatant evil of abortion that kills them.[22]

In the weeks after Dobson issued that statement, Republican governors and attorneys general in Louisiana, Oklahoma, and Alabama also prohibited abortion, deeming it an elective medical procedure during the novel COVID-19 outbreak.[23] But judges blocked most of those orders from being enforced. On April 20, Texas won an appeal of a lower court order, allowing it to keep its ban on abortion as health care workers grapple with the COVID-19 pandemic. Other states, however, have forged compromises, prohibiting surgical abortions while allowing medication-induced abortion.

"The abortion industry continues to defy state orders and national health directives, putting us all at risk of the deadly COVID-19 virus," Porter said in March. "Until the abortion centers are closed, none of us are safe."[24]

Porter joined with more than one hundred prominent pro-life leaders "in calling on President Trump to shut the door to the coronavirus by shutting the doors of the abortion industry before the virus spreads even farther across state lines and across the country." Other supporters included Tim Wildmon, president of the American Family Association, and Tom DeLay, former majority leader of the US House of Representatives. They were joined by thirty thousand medical professionals at StopTheSpreadRightNow.com.

Chapter 7

WHAT ABOUT HEALTH ISSUES WITH COVID-19?

WE ARE DEALING with many new realities as both Christians and Americans. It seems that we are in uncharted territory. To be honest, it almost seems right out of what the Bible said would be coming in the latter days. Everyone is adjusting to new terms, such as *social distancing*, a rapidly changing and volatile economy, and an uncertain future in light of the COVID-19 pandemic. Many of us have battled with feeling scared or worried and are facing a loss of a job or income. Is this the new normal? Or will this just be a season? These are questions even some of America's top faith leaders are praying about and asking the Lord right now.

One of the few times I went grocery shopping, I noticed that most grocery stores were out of many staple items, thanks to the virus. I had never seen anything like that before except for when I endured a few hurricanes down here in Florida. This is different. This is all over the nation—all over the world. We all had a hard time finding toilet paper, fresh meat, canned goods, hand sanitizer, cleaning supplies, rice, and flour as this panic has continued to grow.

At this time more than ever, the importance of living out biblical faith while also taking the findings of those in the medical field seriously has become increasingly clear. Jim Bakker must have felt the same because on February 6, just days before the World Health Organization declared the coronavirus spread a "Public Health Emergency of International Concern" and a month before COVID-19 was declared a pandemic, he talked about it on his show.

Some of Bakker's critics, who never miss an opportunity to bash him, have done so again, mainly online, over COVID-19.

His guest on *The Jim Bakker Show* on February 12 (just as everyone was beginning to talk about this new Chinese virus) was Dr. Sherrill Sellman, a board-certified integrative naturopathic doctor. They had recorded the show six days earlier and talked about Silver Solution, a product Bakker has offered for more than ten years.

After his humiliation with the collapse of the PTL Network, Bakker has supported his ministry not only through donations but by offering Christian books and resources he believes in. Silver Solution is known to boost immunity, and I've used it myself. Bakker and Sellman began the program (which you can see online) that day by saying the product had not yet been tested on this new coronavirus, yet the implication was that it would strengthen your immune system. Somehow that was twisted into accusations that Bakker was selling a cure for coronavirus, and the fake news media went crazy. People suddenly remembered Bakker went to prison in the 1980s, and now they were saying this "huckster" was at it again.

In hindsight it would have been better for Bakker and his guest not to have mentioned the word *coronavirus* on the same show as a health product. But the virus was new, and I assume Bakker thought he was being helpful. The attorney general of Missouri issued a cease and desist order. Bakker complied and even offered to refund money, but that didn't satisfy his critics. The internet suddenly exploded with condemnations of Bakker. Finally I decided to write an op-ed on Charisma News setting the record straight.

I opined that from my perspective of covering him for four decades, I believe Jim Bakker is a sincere man who merely wants to spread the gospel and help people. Has he made mistakes? He's the first to admit it. And he's paid a high price for those mistakes. I believe the Lord has humbled him.

This controversy over Silver Solution is just one account of how the media have targeted Christians and ministries during this time to continue their anti-God narrative and secular, progressive attacks.

Eventually the COVID-19 pandemic will end, this controversy will finally be settled, and I believe Jim will also be fully vindicated. I also believe he's right to emphasize how a strong immune system contributes to good health, just like my friend Dr. Don Colbert, a Spirit-filled medical doctor and Charisma House author. Dr. Colbert is just one of a host of Christians right now in medicine, basic research, and public health who are using their God-given gifts to understand and fight this disease.

I believe strongly that God has given us a powerful and miraculous immune system to fight off the possible trillions of viruses in the world. Many of today's processed foods and GMOs directly target our immune system. This only solidifies the case to build our immunity and practice wisdom in our eating habits.

Dr. Colbert told me that, first of all, as Christians we must approach this pandemic with faith and not fear. We must pray Psalm 91 over ourselves and our families: "Surely He shall deliver you from the snare of the hunter and from the deadly pestilence" (Ps. 91:3).

"Read the Word out loud over yourself and your family every day, and then receive that word by faith and don't live in fear," Colbert said. I would add that we should plead the blood of Jesus over ourselves and our loved ones each day and truly put on the full armor of God. After all, in many ways this is what we have trained for.

But that doesn't mean that following practical advice isn't important. And understanding some basics of how viruses operate will alleviate some of our fears about the coronavirus. In the early days of the pandemic we knew little about the symptoms or how the virus was spread or even how bad it would be. For example, some people freaked out over having a runny nose or productive cough, not realizing they likely didn't have the coronavirus, which produces a dry cough.

As the virus news started to spread, many people felt they may have had it. But most of it was psychosomatic. I remember hearing Vice President Pence say in one of his briefings that nine out of ten people tested for the virus (fearing they had it) tested negative. But people became increasingly worried, and some even panicked over regular cold or flu-like symptoms. At the time, testing was not easily accessible, and people had been listening to the dire predictions of the news and the media's apocalyptic models.

Many had felt that President Trump was going to use his Emergency Powers Act authority to close down the country, but instead, he set up a task force that consequently gave Americans a set of guidelines to follow and empowered the states and local governments in accordance with the Constitution and intentions of the founding fathers. Initially the guidelines were meant to be for fifteen days, but they ended up being for forty-five days to slow the spread.

During one of the initial Coronavirus Task Force meetings, President Trump made a stark announcement that several therapeutic drugs had been showing promising results in the initial testing and clinical trials. One of those drugs was an antimalarial drug that has been on the market and FDA approved for decades: hydroxychloroquine.

But why were some Democratic leaders purposely making it harder for hydroxychloroquine even to be administered in their states? For example, let's look at Nevada governor Steve Sisolak's recent emergency regulation order.[1] He signed an order limiting the use of the two anti-malaria drugs to treat coronavirus patients after President Donald Trump spoke about the possible treatments in several Coronavirus Task Force pressers. Then Michigan governor Gretchen Whitmer followed suit. These orders were eventually rewritten and amended after substantial public backlash. There was even a Michigan state representative, Karen Whitsett, who attributed her recovery from COVID-19 to hydroxychloroquine, and she thanked President Trump for making her aware of it.[2]

The question is, Why would Democrats want to stop the flow of a possible effective treatment to their citizens? Most likely for political purposes, it seems. They just don't want to give the president a win. They even referred to the treatment as "snake oil" even though several studies and medical journals from France, Italy, and China show promising and effective results. Meanwhile, India and other countries limited hydroxychloroquine from being sent out of their countries to other countries. President Trump eventually worked hard to construct a deal with both India and Israel to have millions of doses sent to the United States. It seems the polarization of the American political climate has hit new levels, as even in a pandemic situation there can't seem to be agreement on getting fast and effective medication help to the people.

There are also several vaccines in the works as well as plasma treatments—each showing promise. Very ill coronavirus patients treated with the Ebola drug remdesivir are also showing promising—and quick—results, according to a new report. A very early glimpse into one clinical trial site, at the University of Chicago Medical Center, reveals that most of the patients treated with the medication went home in as little as six days, STAT News reported.

As part of two phase 3 clinical trials—sponsored by the drug's manufacturer, Gilead Sciences—the hospital recruited 125 people with COVID-19, 113 with severe cases, according to the report.

Each patient had been treated with daily infusions of remdesivir, which works by shutting off the bug's ability to replicate inside cells. All these new treatments are still developing as I write this in April, and we are praying and believing for an answer in the weeks and months ahead.

Christian organizations such as Samaritan's Purse also stepped into high gear, and that organization constructed an Emergency Field Hospital in Central Park, which opened on April 1, 2020, to care for those suffering from COVID-19. "We have admitted 120 patients since we opened and, in general, are treating around 50 patients at any given time," said Franklin Graham, CEO of the Billy Graham Evangelistic Association and of Samaritan's Purse, an international Christian relief organization.[3]

"This is a battle—a battle against the disease," said Dr. Elliott Tenpenny, director of the Samaritan's Purse International Health Unit. Tenpenny is serving in New York City and has been instrumental in spearheading much of the New York operation for the organization.[4]

The fourteen-tent, sixty-eight-bed respiratory care unit was designed especially for this coronavirus response. Among other notable features, the mobile medical facility includes ten ICU beds equipped with ventilators and needed medical equipment. "Patients are coming to us from our partner, the Mount Sinai Health System, which has, like other healthcare facilities, been overwhelmed by those sickened with the virus."[5]

The coronavirus is also canceling in-person church services all across the nation. Churches are accustomed to hosting weekly gatherings; some even have several services each week.

My longtime friend Joan Hunter is a healing minister. Just as officials were beginning to quarantine the population, I recorded a podcast with her about how Christians can walk in divine health.

She said that first of all, we must be people of faith. It's almost shocking to think how quickly this unknown virus overtook everyone's attention. At first the Chinese government worked hard to cover it up, but as it began to spread rapidly across the globe, entire nations panicked.

"The Word says perfect love casts out all fear—not most fear, *all* fear," she said. "We must not fear. As I was getting ready this morning, I kept hearing over and over in my head, 'I've got this. I've got this.' Then I would hear, 'God's got this.'"

Joan believes there's going to be a greater emphasis on praying for the sick in the near future. But if God's people haven't practiced praying for the sick and haven't learned wisdom, this will be difficult.

I live in a part of the country not hard-hit by the coronavirus, but it became personal when someone I know, Greg Mundis, executive director of Assemblies of God World Missions (AGWM), got the coronavirus. His wife contracted the disease shortly afterward. Interestingly the couple have been using a new drug on the market. Thankfully they both recovered.

When Mundis tested positive for COVID-19, AGWM shared a call to prayer on Facebook, saying: "BREAKING NEWS AND CALL TO PRAYER: AGWM Executive Director Greg Mundis has been positively confirmed as having COVID-19. We ask everyone to intercede for Greg in this crucial time—for complete healing of his lungs and kidneys, and for the Spirit of God to fill his hospital room with God's healing presence."[6]

I had the privilege of speaking to his son, Dr. Greg Mundis Jr., who is an orthopedic surgeon from San Diego. I invited him on my podcast, where he shared with me what it was like for both of his parents to get sick with COVID-19. Greg told me that his father hosted several French delegates at the Assemblies of God headquarters, and they held a few meetings together. When the delegates returned home, they began feeling ill, and Greg's father followed suit not too long afterward. When the delegates were told they tested positive for COVID-19, Greg's dad knew he had to get tested too.

"Monday morning my dad went through a drive-through testing center to get tested and was feeling very ill at that point," Greg said. "My mom was really worried about him by the time he got home. The EMS was called, an ambulance took him to the hospital, and about four to five hours later he was on a ventilator."

Both of Greg's parents took hydroxychloroquine, which seemed to help. As discussed earlier, hydroxychloroquine is typically used to treat malaria, but it can also be used to treat and mitigate lupus and arthritis. As I write this, the FDA is still testing it as a treatment against COVID-19 and hopefully will learn soon if it's as effective as early users testify it is.

President Trump recently touted the drug as a potential cure for the coronavirus, which has given the medicine quite a bit of press lately. Some have criticized Trump for encouraging the use of this drug, while others see it as practically a miracle medicine.

"It's not a miracle drug," Dr. Mundis told me. "You know, the miracle drug is staying home and not infecting other people. If we all do that, then the miracle's done, ironically. So yes, the drug has been used. It has FDA clearance for rheumatologic diseases and in the antimalarial arena, and it's been used in this setting [of COVID-19] somewhat successfully by these published reports. So it's off-label use, but right now, it seems to be the best tool we have to fight this virus from a medical standpoint."

Greg encouraged Christians to see God, not this antimalarial drug, as their Savior in the COVID-19 pandemic. For those who feel stuck at home during quarantine, he said they can use that time to press deeper in to God.

To me, that is good advice. The medical community and the politicians won't encourage this, but as Christians we must ask what God is saying. The most important thing is to not let fear take root in our hearts. As Christians we have been trained for a time such as this. We are made to overcome in Jesus Christ. This too shall pass. Let's do what the Bible says and pray for those who are sick and believe they will indeed be healed.

Chapter 8

WHAT IS GOD SAYING TO HIS PROPHETS?

I OPENED THIS BOOK with the amazing prophecy David Wilkerson gave more than thirty years ago. He shared this word with my friend Mike Evans, who happened upon it only recently. Mike told me he picked up his Bible one day, and a handwritten note about his conversation with the late evangelist David Wilkerson fell out. The message it contained shook Mike to his knees.

Wilkerson became famous on the mean streets of New York in 1958, when he began ministering to gang members and drug addicts. He later started Teen Challenge, which now has 1,400 affiliate centers in over 129 nations around the globe. But despite his beginnings, Wilkerson is better known today as a prophet who warned people in a bold and unafraid manner about the truth of God's Word in order to draw them to Jesus. He had a unique gift mix—a prophet with the heart of an evangelist—which made for a radical, soul-winning, weeping prophet.

I followed his ministry closely over the years, having been impacted as a teenager by reading his best-known book, *The Cross and the Switchblade*. I also know that not all of his prophecies came to pass. But I was deeply moved when Mike, founder of the Friends of Zion Museum in Jerusalem, told me about a prophecy of Wilkerson's that came to light recently—nine years after his death.

The handwritten note was from a meeting Mike had with Wilkerson—or Brother Dave, as Mike refers to him—at the Embassy Suites near the Dallas-Fort Worth airport in 1986.

It was a prophetic word Wilkerson gave Mike, who wrote it down and stuck it in the Bible he used at the time. It stayed there until Mike found it not long ago. The prophecy said: "I see a plague coming on the world and the bars, church, and government shut down. The plague will hit New York City and shake it like it has never been shaken. The plague is going to force prayerless believers into radical prayer, into their Bibles and repentance will be the cry from true men of God in the pulpit. And out of it will come a third Great Awakening that will sweep America and the world."[1]

Mike did a widely distributed video sermon telling about this prophecy and then included it in his book *A Great Awakening Is Coming* which released on April 16, 2020. Immediately people online began saying Wilkerson never said it. There was no proof. It was a private conversation. Someone told me some of Wilkerson's family members were making it seem as if Mike made it up. So I decided to email his son Gary, whom I've known over the years. He replied: "I have read the post and we at World Challenge have no written quotes exactly like the one circulating widely, [though] I do feel it could very well be something my father would have said." That was good enough for me to include in this book, especially since Mike Evans and I have been good friends for many years, and I absolutely trust his word.

But how could something so terrible lead to an awakening of that magnitude? Mike said this is how God often works. The first two Great Awakenings came around times of hardship.

"The two Great Awakenings that America has [had that shook] the entire nation happened around the time of the American Revolution and the Civil War," he said. "The pilgrims came to this country on fire for God, but their children didn't. Their children became cold in their souls. And America started pushing away. And then all of a sudden, here comes this manifested Great Awakening that shook the nation. And then you had the American Revolution. You had another one, and you had the Civil War. And I thought, 'Wow, [Wilkerson] said there's going to be a third Great Awakening.'"

Could it be that this COVID-19 pandemic we're experiencing is the trial that will usher in the next Great Awakening? Mike said for that awakening to happen, God needs to uproot idols from this nation.

"People have taken and allowed things to become their idols; money and materialism has become an idol; their success and…reputation has become an idol," he said.

He believes that for some in America who strongly support President Trump, their devotion to him has become like an idol. Even this must go. God demands our whole hearts and nothing less. "I think that God is shaking us because He's taken all of our security away," Mike said. "All the things that [made us] comfortable [must be] removed."

Outside certain Christian circles, few pay much attention to prophecy, but these times are different. Even Fox News reported in March 2020 on a prophecy from rising prophetic voice Shawn Bolz, who said at the time that the Lord had shown him the end of the coronavirus.[2] I reported on March 9 about what I considered Fox's evenhanded treatment and was shocked it was my biggest podcast ever—by more than double.[3]

Later when I did a second podcast and interviewed Shawn, he told me that the response to the story about him on Fox News had been incredible. If nothing else, this shows that people are hungry for God, perhaps even more so now that COVID-19 is wreaking havoc.

Shawn's prophecy had two major points. The first is that the enemy will flee as the church rises up. God has called the church to respond to COVID-19, not sit back passively and merely let it happen. "God's going to turn the tide of this thing," he said.

The second point of the word is that millions will not die from this. Fox News chose not to report this, Shawn told me.

"I prophesied that this will not become a pandemic with pandemonium and millions dying," he said. "Tens of millions won't die worldwide, and millions won't die in America."

When we talked, Shawn said that almost every day major news sources were citing a health professional who claimed between twenty million and sixty million people worldwide would die from COVID-19.[4] Long before the medical experts began lowering their estimates of the death toll, Shawn said this will not happen. Time will tell how many lives will be lost as a result of COVID-19, but as I write this in April, Dr. Anthony Fauci, a key member of the president's Coronavirus Task Force, says it appears the US death toll will be well under one hundred thousand, a far cry from the more than two million deaths predicted without social distancing.[5]

"You have people who work alongside the World Health Organization (WHO)…saying, 'We're going down the doomsday road,'" he said. "Then you have the prophetic community and the church saying, 'That's not where we're going. That's not God's story for our generation.' And that's even more important than how fast it turns, is that God has a story for our generation, and it's not to take out a whole generation of people to purge or do something. That's not a prophetic word from God or God's desire."

Shawn said WHO doesn't have the full equation. God wants to bring medical and scientific advancements that will move society forward. That could even include a cure for cancer.

But how will this pandemic affect the church? Shawn believes it will only serve to give the church greater ground.

"The church has been last in line [in the media space]," he told me. "And God wants to give the church media space and social media space and internet real estate. That's just as important as their natural places they meet in. This is a training ground right now for the church to respond."

Instead of churches just putting information up online, God is going to move churches to actually engage, build community, and foster connection online, Shawn said. Churches that want to remain only information-focused in the online space will eventually disappear.

"It's a preparation for an entire revival that we would have all of our technology in order and the practice that we need because God's going to bring half of the revival—it's going to happen virtually," he said. "And the second thing is that I believe right now there's about to be an economic upturn, not downturn. I believe the Lord showed me that Trump would win another term in office.

"I saw the financial condition of our economy," Shawn said. "And in the second or third—by the end of the second year and beginning of the third year of [Trump's] next four years in office, we're going to hit one of the greatest times, if not the greatest time, of economic stability in our history. That's setting us up for the next twenty years."

That's encouraging, but what are other prophetic voices saying?

From his powerful new book *The Passover Prophecies*, well-respected prophet and friend Chuck D. Pierce states that as of late August 2019 the church has entered a "Passover decade," which will test the world and the church like no time in recent memory. In fact, in September 2019 the Lord spoke to Pierce, saying that starting in early 2020:

> This will be a year that plague-like conditions will infiltrate the earth. This Passover will be a modern-day Passover like the initial Passover where My people were redeemed from Egypt. If a

remnant in a nation will celebrate My blood and press through after Passover for the next forty days, I will restore, remake, realign, reset, and recalibrate their future! This will be a year that I begin the process of separating and dividing nations that belong to Me. This division will start at Passover and then continue through the decade.

I know Chuck Pierce is a man of integrity. I believe he hears from God. He also speaks in mystical terms, such as "moving from this season to the next season God has." I believe that people who really have a heart after the deep things of God long to hear what God is saying and to understand it. I've learned you must have a discerning spirit to understand what the Spirit is saying. Chuck seems to have a gift of helping people move into those realms and as a result has developed a huge following. I've had the privilege of speaking at one of Chuck's conferences. I remember that years ago he was prophesying things about China becoming dominant in the world, which at the time seemed a little far-fetched to me, but we are seeing it come true.

There are internet watchdogs who monitor everything Chuck says, most recently about whether he saw in September or January that a plague was coming that would test us until Passover. Because I am including that in this book, I researched what he said.

First, I know Chuck is accurate because when he visited me and Joy in Lake Mary in early 2008, he told us at a restaurant over lunch that Barack Obama would be elected for two terms but he didn't feel he should release that publicly. Years later Chuck remembered that conversation exactly as Joy and I did—even to how Joy reacted to his word.

I told that prophecy in both *God and Donald Trump* and *God, Trump, and the 2020 Election*. In both books I discussed "the prophetic" extensively and talked about it in the media widely and have received no pushback. I think it is because deep down even secular people want to understand what God is saying.

I knew before Passover that both Shawn Bolz and Chuck Pierce were using it as a pivotal date. Even before I learned of some anti-Charismatic online trolls bashing them after Easter because the plague didn't go away. I came to understand that they were saying the plague wouldn't be as bad as people said. As I write this, I saw on television that President Trump was remarking that the death toll appears to top out somewhere above sixty thousand deaths, which is a far cry from the two million deaths being predicted in February and early March. Also, some were saying back then this pandemic may last until the fall. As this goes to press, I know time will tell when it ends. In fact, I'm not sure how to know "it ends." Like the Spanish flu a decade ago, it stays with us but in a less deadly way, and we learn to live with it.

I believe God's prophets were saying it wouldn't be as bad as the politicians, medical experts, and liberal media were saying. And that something would happen around Passover—and it did. It was right during that time—as noted by Frank Amedia earlier—that the virus in New York peaked, and the numbers of daily deaths began to decline. It became obvious by then that this wasn't as bad as something like the bubonic plague and it began to "flatten out."

If you understand prophecy, it's often symbolic and vague. People did not recognize the messianic prophecies applied to Jesus while He walked on earth. In 1 Corinthians 13 the apostle Paul says that "now we see through a glass darkly," and to me that explains why prophets don't always see future events as crystal clear as 2020 hindsight.

Because I trust Chuck's prophetic insights, when a trusted colleague told me that back in September Chuck had received a prophetic word about a plague-like invasion that would hit leading up

to Passover, I repeated it on a podcast in mid-March without veri-
fying it. I had seen a newsletter from his ministry in January saying
the same thing. But before we went to press, I did some more dig-
ging and began to understand he made the prophecy privately in
September and made it publicly in January, referring back to when
God spoke it to his heart. At my request, his ministry let me see
some notes of meetings in which they wrote what they felt God
was saying. There was an August 2, 2019, memo and the words
"Passover" and "modern day plague." I know that Chuck probably
didn't fully understand what would transpire, and he wasn't taking
notes to prove later what he said. But he has the integrity to show me
the notes because he has nothing to hide. Whether it was September
or January, I think the prophetic word was pretty incredible. It's as
Jesus said in Mark 4:23: "If anyone has ears to hear, let him hear."

I'm so grateful for people such as Shawn and Chuck, who are
standing up and speaking prophetically despite the media's contrary
narrative. Sadly, however, it's not just the media that pushes against
prophecy. Many self-proclaimed biblical "experts" who don't believe
in modern-day prophecy love to pick apart anything that supports
their position that the Charismatic gifts are not for today. That,
however, is certainly not my position.

I only hope that the church will choose to heed these godly
prophets instead of the media, which seem to have a different
agenda.

Regardless of what is to come, we know one thing is for sure: the
hour is getting later. We also know God's heart is to see us repent
as a nation and as a church. In Christ we have a promise not only
of "a future and a hope" (Jer. 29:11) but that all the promises of God
are "yes" and "amen" (2 Cor. 1:20). This is why it's crucial that we
understand the spiritual aspects of the COVID-19 pandemic and
how this could lead to a great move of God.

Chapter 9

UNDERSTANDING THE SPIRITUAL ASPECTS OF COVID-19

AN ENTIRE SECTION of my book *God, Trump, and the 2020 Election* is about "Understanding the Spiritual Realm." Even though I was trained as a secular journalist at the University of Florida, as a believer I see everything from a biblical worldview. To me that means God created all things, and there is an unseen spiritual realm as real as the physical world we see. I agree with my friend the late John Paul Jackson, who quoted French philosopher Pierre Teilhard de Chardin: "We are not human beings having a temporary spiritual experience; we are spiritual beings having a temporary human experience."[1]

I also believe there is spiritual warfare at work in our world. And if we understand that, many of the things that otherwise don't make sense are understandable. I've spent my career reporting on the Christian community, the spiritual world, and God's end-time plan for man. Readers who know me through *Charisma* magazine, listen to my *Strang Report* podcast, or who have read my other books on Trump know this and won't be surprised that I include a chapter here trying to discern what all this means spiritually.

As I have written from the start, it has never been about Donald J. Trump. Although many like to critique, criticize, and analyze his every move, this really isn't what God is concerned about at all! What happened in 2016 was a direct response to the prayers of the righteous here in America and beyond. It was a last-minute reprieve!

It was a period where God was willing to show His mercy, His grace, and His love and give us just a little more time.

The time was given not only to the American people but more so to the American church! Our mandate was simple: *Do not* act as if it's business as usual. God wanted us to repent as a nation and as a church! To begin to lead the culture again in accordance with the truth of the Word of God. To once again stand for righteousness and push back against the demonic agenda we were under so we could change the trajectory in which this nation was headed. At that time, we had seen decades of moral decline, a prolonged anti-God/anti-Christianity movement, and a death culture that continued to celebrate the murder of our most innocent societal members—our babies! Has any of this changed?

Now, as we look back at the last four years, has the American church done its part of the bargain? Have we risen up in prayer, fasting, and standing for righteousness? Have we been outspoken from the pulpit and pushed back against the assignment of the enemy to morally bankrupt our culture and attack our children's minds and identities? Have we made progress in taking our country back from falling off the moral abyss? Have we done enough?

I believe the moment of truth will soon be upon us, as there are two very different possible scenarios ahead. They are as follows:

1. We could see the president fully vindicated in each and every accusation, attack, and plan that was devised by those who have opposed him. Not only this, but also we could see large elements of the corrupt shadow government taken down. We could even witness indictments and arrests and finally see "the swamp" truly drained. This would be the best-case scenario. In this possible outcome, there could be a restoration of law and order,

a fresh respect for the Constitution, and peace and prosperity restored to our great nation! This could also usher in a new era of American ingenuity, renaissance, economic growth, and, even more important, a great spiritual awakening and return to morality and biblical values. I pray this is our fate!

2. We could plunge into a period of tremendous unrest. The president could lose the 2020 election and be removed from power. We could see great economic peril and decline resulting in a plummeting of our dollar and global currency hegemony. We also could face immediate international threats from our adversaries, which could lead to an outright war.

In addition to these things, there could even be an escalating civil unrest here at home. People could take to the streets in protest. Even with a somewhat smooth transition of power, the change in leadership could be enough to sink our forward trajectory, as there are many sensitive variables at stake. The whole situation is a massive powder keg.

There is also a third option where the president wins in 2020—stays in power—and yet we still see tremendous turbulence and unrest, as the spiritual battle between light and darkness rages on for the heart and future of America!

What does it all mean?

I am concerned that if Trump loses, our reprieve as a nation and church could be over. God has given us four years of grace so we could be about His business! If that grace period comes to an end, I believe that will be a direct rebuke to the church and the fact that we didn't do enough, despite the tremendous grace He showed us. Instead, we in fact did continue with business as usual and basically lost our blessing period, ushering in a period of great sorrow and woes, maybe even worse than the Great Depression.

Although both scenarios depicted are not only fluid but subject to change and to be looked at through the lens of our own beliefs, views, and interpretation, I cannot stress enough the importance of the time period we are in right now! God responds directly to the prayers of the righteous! We have seen this consistently throughout the Bible and history. What we do right now is utterly important! Will we respond in a manner that pleases the Lord?

Many Christians have not even understood the importance and spiritual relevance of this reprieve season of grace. Instead of activating, many have been focused on the wrong things or remained in a spiritual stupor. Others have looked to the president to make the needed changes. This question is, Have we really done what God has asked of us? Is it too late already? Or can we still step up and make our impact now? To those reading this book today, this is no mistake. God has placed this message heavily on my heart for a reason! His question remains: Will you respond? I believe the ball is in our court as a church body. This is a moment of great decision. What we do and what happens next will determine a lot. Our very future is at stake.

Now, with COVID-19, which almost no one saw coming, I'm interested that a few modern-day Christian leaders who have been gifted to hear from God did see a plague on the horizon. One was Chuck Pierce—as I've mentioned in the last chapter—who saw as far back as 2008 that God would use the "trump card," which he later interpreted as meaning Donald Trump would one day be president.

In September 2019, just as I was finishing *God, Trump, and the 2020 Election*, Chuck prophesied (and wrote) that word saying the "nations would come into turmoil until Passover" (April 8–16, 2020).[2] It's one of the clearest prophetic words about what we now call COVID-19. Chuck said that around the time of Rosh Hashanah, the beginning of the Jewish New Year, looking at the year ahead.

Some have said he predicted the plague would end by Passover, but he said in writing that it "would test us" through Passover, and it did. Though the pandemic did not end then, Passover seemed to be a turning point.[3]

The Lord showed me that the media and political structures would use COVID-19 to develop political strategies against the covenant restoration of this nation.

It's important we listen to what the prophets are saying about this matter. Even though the media gives us facts, those who listen carefully to God's heart can give us spiritual insight.

Chuck points to two passages in the book of Joel as scriptures that are prophetic for this hour:

> Do not be afraid, land; exult and rejoice, for the LORD has done great things! Do not be afraid, beasts of the field, because the wild pastures flourish, because the tree bears its fruit; the fig tree and the vine yield their abundance. And children of Zion, exult and rejoice in the LORD your God, because He has given to you the early rain for vindication. He showers down rains for you, the early rain and the latter rain, as before.
>
> —JOEL 2:21–23

> Hurry and come, all you surrounding nations, and gather there. Bring down Your warriors, O LORD. Let the nations be roused, and go up to the Valley of Jehoshaphat; for there I will sit to judge all the surrounding nations....Multitudes, multitudes, in the valley of decision! For the day of the LORD is near in the valley of the decision.
>
> —JOEL 3:11–12, 14

I find these scriptures interesting when applied to our global situation today. After all, this virus is affecting the entire world, not just China. That—not his supposed xenophobia—is the real reason President Donald Trump placed a travel ban on all foreign nationals traveling to the United States. He's trying to protect our nation.

When I wrote about this in March as we were hearing scary projections of millions dying, I told my readers to respond to these prophetic words about the coronavirus by praying. Pray scientists can find a vaccine. Pray the church would shine with the light of Jesus in this frightening time. Pray the virus would be contained and wouldn't spread any further. Pray against demonic spirits of fear that would attack the nations.

Pierce says this about China: "A new day is breaking in the (Chinese) church. 'Harvest angels' are being sent to back the army of the Lord and His covenant people. China will be 'the Nation of Dichotomy.' It will have an army set against the purposes of God and His People. At the same time, however, China will send forth the greatest 'Army of Harvesters' the world has ever known."[4]

According to a 2018 report by the Council for Foreign Relations, "China has witnessed a religious revival over the past four decades, in particular with a significant increase in Christian believers. The number of Chinese Protestants has grown by an average of 10 percent annually since 1979. By some estimates, China is on track to have the world's largest population of Christians by 2030."[5]

Think about that startling statistic: The nation that is striving to become the dominant economic power in the world is also seeing an explosion of growth as the persecuted church there continues to thrive. That is true dichotomy!

In March I interviewed missionary Dennis Balcombe about how Christians in China were testifying of being healed of COVID-19. (See chapter 3.) There is no way to verify these testimonies. But I do believe in healing, and most victims of the virus do recover. When I've had the flu in the past, I've asked to be anointed with oil and prayed over, knowing God can speed the healing process.

So far I've dealt with the health advice and the political commentary surrounding COVID-19. Now I want to offer a new perspective—a perspective of healing and spiritual warfare.

On my podcast I recently spoke with Cal Pierce, founder of the Healing Rooms in Spokane, Washington. There are seventy-four countries that have Healing Rooms so far, and God is using those hubs of healing in mighty ways. I invited Cal onto my podcast because I came across a message he posted on Facebook in which he was decreeing healing over the nation.

On Facebook he wrote: "We, as the body of Christ, speak to this mountain of coronavirus. You spirit of death and fear, be taken up and cast back into hell. You will stop now and leave the earth. We decree that in 10 days, the world will acknowledge this turnaround to the glory of God. This is the will of God, established by the blood of Jesus, whose authority you must obey."[6]

His post garnered enormous response with many comments from encouraged believers who were ready to wage spiritual warfare in Jesus' name. Cal says this is the attitude believers must have right now as the nation wrestles with COVID-19. After all, if we stay silent, the enemy will continue with his agenda.

"The enemy has an agenda against our nation—of course, every nation, actually," Cal says. "Of course, our battle isn't in flesh and blood but against principalities. The enemy is trying to take God out of this country."

Cal says that as God has begun to move mightily in this nation—by putting Trump in office and stirring up revivals—the enemy has been trying to thwart His plans. The devil tried to impeach the president, but that didn't work. Now he is using this coronavirus to stir up mass panic and fear in the United States, Cal says.

"I believe it's a test that the enemy is making against God's people, because he wants to turn us from where God has taken us in this hour and…see if we're going to walk in fear," he says. "Because fear will bring punishment."

For that reason Christians must be careful not to give way to that fear and instead stand in faith.

"We are the body of Jesus," Cal says. "He's our head, and we're filled with resurrection power, which gives us authority over all the works of the enemy. I think God's people have to begin to address the truth that makes us free."

But how do we walk in that truth? By choosing to believe God will continue to bring a great awakening to this country.

"So we try to be proactive in these times and seasons and really understand what's going on and what the attack is," Cal says. "It's so easy to set our eyes on the earth. We're in the world, but we're not of it. We're of a kingdom realm. And we need to set our eyes on the things above and realize that God created the world for His kids, and He put us here to fulfill what Jesus wanted to do to bring His kingdom on earth."

In Mid-March 2020 as the "shelter-in-place" orders were just being sent out, US Sen. Marco Rubio, a Republican from Florida, held an urgent briefing for pastors regarding the novel coronavirus and COVID-19. Rubio, a known Christian, briefed pastors and Christian leaders on a conference call, which I was grateful to join.

"It's a reminder that we are advanced creatures because we're created in the image of God, but we're not God," Senator Rubio said. "There are still things—despite all the tools we've invented and all the advances we've made in science—there are still things in the world that we can't control.[7]

"It's an enormous challenge that I think the church has a very important role to play in because right now people are scared," Rubio said. "I think people are dealing with some realizations of the humility we need to have. And one more point I would make is I think people also are being reminded of how trivial so much that we focus on is. A lot of things will suddenly appear very trivial."

Rubio said one crucial way pastors can respond to this need is by ministering to people in creative ways—even via livestream online. With so many feeling isolated, it's also important to do what we can to connect with people, including dropping off meals with a note, picking up groceries for people, or even sending others to check on those living alone.

Prophet and respected author Jeremiah Johnson said he received a prophetic dream about President Donald Trump and the coronavirus (COVID-19). Johnson shared about the dream, which he received on March 16, on one of my recent podcasts.[8]

He said that in the dream, he was taken to a baseball stadium, where he saw a slender man who was demonized standing on the pitcher's mound. In the batter's box was none other than Donald Trump, wearing a pinstripe New York Yankees jersey with the number 3 on it. Johnson immediately recognized that as Babe Ruth's number.

When he looked at the scoreboard, Johnson saw the count was 3 and 2—and Trump was two strikes in.

"I knew in the dream that the demon-possessed pitcher intended to throw a fastball right past Donald for a strikeout," Johnson said. "As I held my breath and watched the pitch come out, I was suddenly stunned to watch the ball be slowed down by a supernatural force in the air. And by the time the ball got to Trump, it was going very slowly, and he hit the ball out of the park for a big home run.

"In the dream I heard the voice of God say, 'The enemy has

intended to strike out Donald Trump at a very critical hour in history. But behold, supernatural help is on the way, for I will slow down the advancement of the enemy and allow him to knock this out of the park. For it is simply a matter of time before the victory,'" Johnson said.

He woke up with an incredible sense of peace.[9]

I find Johnson's dream profound, especially considering we are in a time in history like no other. Never before has everything shut down the way it has in so many countries, including many states in the United States.

And Johnson isn't alone in his encouraging prophecies about the coronavirus. Thankfully, others such as Shawn Bolz, Kenneth Copeland, and Chuck Pierce are prophesying a swift end to this virus. They're also saying this COVID-19 outbreak isn't going to be as bad as everyone predicted.

Time will tell, certainly. As of May 3, 2020, just before this book went to press, the coronavirus had killed more than sixty-six thousand people in the United States.[10] And as of April 23 it was reported that more than twenty-six million Americans had filed for unemployment. According to MarketWatch, "The spike in unemployment has likely pushed the jobless rate to between 15% and 20%, economists estimate. The only other time in American history when unemployment was that high was in the early stages of the Great Depression almost a century ago."[11]

But I believe God will show this country mercy—just as He showed us mercy by giving us Trump as a president when we least deserved it. Many other Christians around the nation and I believe God raised up Trump for such a time as this.

Jeremiah Johnson sees a window of time that God has given the American people for a divine reset.

"There's a real recipe for awakening, especially in America," he says.

"Some of the greatest gods—sports, entertainment—are being shut down. Schools are being closed, which is forcing needed relational proximity for marriages and families. Large churches and conferences are being canceled, which allows for house-to-house gatherings like the book of Acts. So I believe around the time of Passover, we're going to see [the virus] really slow down, but I believe in the midst of this, there's a divine reset. There's a recipe for awakening."[12]

Chapter 10

FOR CHRISTIANS, WHAT DOES THIS ALL MEAN?

IN THESE UNSETTLING times what good can all these problems bring? If you're a Christian, they may point to an awakening—a turning toward God not only in America but around the world.

Rev. Kevin Jessip, president of the Global Strategic Alliance, believes a tsunami of the Holy Spirit is beginning to flow, bringing with it overwhelming fruit, dreams, visions, signs, wonders, miracles, and all manner of spiritual gifts.

"We are on the verge of the greatest move of God in all the ages. This outpouring will sweep multitudes into the kingdom of God as they are saved, healed, and delivered," Kevin said. "Spiritual leaders from around the world are sensing this wave. This sovereign move of God is rising, and through the power of the Holy Spirit, there is a new unity being woven within the fabric of the body of Christ."

Kevin should know. He's a great networker, and he's working with church leaders across the globe to call for repentance. This is what 2 Chronicles 7:14 is talking about when it says we must humble ourselves, pray, and seek God's face, believing that as we repent and turn, God's response will be to hear from heaven, forgive our sins, and heal our land.

For those who have spiritual eyes, Kevin explains it this way: "Our foundation is in our identity in Christ bought by His blood on Calvary's cross and through the finished work of His sacrifice. Since the Spirit of God incarnated Immanuel and entered history from eternity in Jesus of Nazareth, the receding tide was reversed.

This was the beginning of the greatest outpouring since creation was born. As an earthquake at the bottom of the ocean produces a tsunami, so the birth of Jesus the Messiah shook the very foundations of hell."

Kevin says Jesus' incarnation, life, death, resurrection, and ascension were like an earthquake. Then before He went to heaven, Jesus told His disciples to go to Jerusalem, Judea, Samaria, and the uttermost parts of the earth and make disciples. (See Matthew 28:18–20; Acts 1:8.) That happened in the first few centuries after the birth of the church, and the power of the Holy Spirit that fell in the upper room on the Day of Pentecost is still at work on the earth almost two millennia later.

As Spirit-filled believers we know God is still healing the sick and raising the dead. The power and gifts of the Holy Spirit have been at work uninterrupted throughout church history and have continued even into this present day.

Kevin told me that one of the Greek words translated "opportunity" in the Scriptures is *kairos*. It implies the right moment, that which lasts only for a while.[1] *Kairos* means a God-given opportunity is being offered to mankind at a specific moment in time. However, the word also implies there is a risk—of faith. In other words, as time moves on, we can miss the opportunity.

We are living in a *kairos* moment today. First Corinthians 14:8 says, "If the trumpet makes an uncertain sound, who will prepare himself for the battle?" This verse is warning us that now is our personal *kairos*. Like the men from the tribe of Issachar who had "understanding of times" (1 Chron. 12:32), we are called to understand our times and seize the moment.

Kevin also pointed out that the word *opportunity* comes from the Latin phrase *ob portum veniens*, which means "coming toward a port."[2] He said in the ancient world seamen used the term to describe the time when the tide and winds were favorable to make it safely to port. When that moment came, they would set their sails to take full advantage.[3] In the same way, when God is at work, as He is now, we must wake up to that opportunity, set our sails to His favor, and ride in His boat, using the wind and tide.

The Holy Spirit's anointing does not flow without conditions. It continues and increases through the same process that secured it at first: unceasing prayer to God. We must count all else loss and failure without it. His holy oil only fills praying hearts.

Prayer is the sole condition to maintain this anointing, which pervades the spirit, convicts the conscience, and breaks the heart. There are now rumblings as never before of the Spirit's outpouring as in the promised latter rain. The Lord is arising for the sake of His name, infusing His bride with a habitation of His Holy Spirit, where there is no fear as she enters His rest.

The time has come for each of us; we have been called to seize the moment! We are at the threshold of the greatest move of God in our time. Though the time of God's favor has been generously extended to all people at all times through the cross, church historians have noted specific seasons of God's increased favor throughout history.

Scholars use terms such as *outpouring, awakening, movement,* and *revival* to describe those unique periods when God bestowed His grace and power in unusual measure upon a people to extend His kingdom on earth. Anything other than a Nineveh-type move of repentance will not move us forward in the battle for the soul of our nation or any nation.

We must seize the moment. Carpe diem—seize the day! Seize the God-given opportunity. The Scriptures say God will "do exceedingly abundantly beyond all that we ask or imagine, according to the power that works in us" (Eph. 3:20). However, for that to happen, we must be men and women of action who are ready to respond by faith to what God has initiated. As Paul said, we must "walk carefully, not as fools, but as wise men, making the most of the time because the days are evil" (Eph. 5:15–16).

The Return, a sacred solemn assembly called by Messianic Rabbi Jonathan Cahn, will take place September 26, 2020, on the National Mall in Washington, DC. The gathering will include ten days of prayer and repentance September 18–28.[4] I'm honored to be part of the steering committee.

Kevin is among those who issued the call for The Return, and he has written extensively about his passion for the church and for a great awakening in our day. One essay was so powerful I wanted to close the book with its insights. Kevin gave me permission to include it here:

> The waters and waves around us are rocky. The storm is here. It seems as though we are in grave danger. What will we do?
>
> For many years we've been comfortable. Even when we thought we weren't, we were.... We have forgotten what real trials and tests are, as it's been over a generation since the American church has truly been tested in such a capacity.
>
> Here we are now. How will we respond? Will we panic? Will we lose hope? Will we be like the children of Israel, who forgot what God did in freeing them from captivity? Will we instead shine?
>
> We have a choice. That choice is clear. This is our boat moment.
>
> The storm is all around us, but what we have forgotten is we have the King of kings and Lord of lords sitting in the boat with us.
>
> He alone has the power to calm the wind and the seas. He has the power to give us the peace that passes all understanding. What place does fear have with love?

The waves may get worse. The thunder may rage. Many will panic. Some will say this is the end, but the end is not here yet.

Our gadgets can't save us. Our technology can't save us. Our big buildings can't save us. Celebrities can't help either. All the money in the world will do us no good right now. You see, we are simply in a boat.

This can be our greatest hour. This is what we have trained for. Without faith it is impossible to please Him, but *with* faith, we can move that mountain! Let's stop with our apathy. Let's die to our flesh. Let's deny our fears and say no to our doubts. We have eternal hope. We have the absolute truth. We have His everlasting word. And we have Jesus—in the boat with us right now.

Conclusion

IT'S NEVER BEEN ABOUT TRUMP

I ADMIT, I'M UNASHAMEDLY supportive of the president in *Charisma* and in the books I've written. But it is not my job to be his apologist. Donald Trump may be a somewhat crass New Yorker, one who sounds like many CEOs I have met in my lifetime. He may not be careful with his words and often speaks his mind without a filter. He certainly does have skeletons in his closet and has done things over the years that his enemies use to keep his audacious life and lifestyle consistently on the front pages of the corporate-controlled news outlets. Others outright hate him. But let's dive a little deeper into the details.

Have you seen the moral degradation that has taken place in our nation over the last fifty years? The breakdown of the family unit? The rise of the "medicated generation"? The massive sexualization of our society and young people? What about their identity crisis? How about the explosion of pornography? What about the largest wealth transfer in the history of the world from West to East? And how did China get so much of our secret technology? Stealth/missiles?

All the while, the wealth gap here at home between the rich and poor has gotten wider, while the size of the American middle class has been greatly diminished. Manufacturing left, and we became a service-based economy. As this all happened, our debt became unpayable and unsustainable, while our dollar lost much of its intrinsic value.

Have you wondered why these things have taken place as if they were all almost orchestrated in a completely planned sequence of events as if someone were planning our slow demise?

What if I were to tell you these events were planned? What if I were to tell you that powerful ungodly groups actually control/own much of the "mainstream" media, the central banks, and many of the world's largest corporations and that they all were working in tandem toward an agenda? I know, it sounds crazy, but I believe it's actually true! Even the UN was founded by some of those very same elites. Look up its history. Now the UN Agenda 2020 and Agenda 2030 clearly lay out this go-forward plan for us all to see. It is slowly pushing us toward globalization. The UN wants people to be all mixed with no borders or national identities. This is their strategy.

Christians should discern this, as it's all laid out for us in the Bible. Clearly this is the "beast system" being finalized and prepared for the next phase. Money is going digital. People are getting used to chips. A massive 5G network is in its final stages. And now China is cracking down on Christians and giving its citizens a "social score" that determines if they are good socialist communists or not. If not, the government greatly restricts their rights. Sound familiar? Oh yes, companies such as Google, Facebook, and others are already helping China to do this and are ready to roll out a similar system right here at home in the not-so-distant future. People may claim this is all conspiracy, yet I believe it's all very possible. You can study it for yourself!

There is a powerful military industrial complex that needs perpetual war to continue its global dominance, power structure, and rule. President Dwight D. Eisenhower warned us of this very entity. The Deep State is the unelected officials often referred to as the "shadow government" that controls the military industrial complex and its many tentacles. This is why we have seen constant war for years now and why we have seen regime change in so many nations around the world. There are only three nations left that are not under the central banking system: North Korea, Iran, and Cuba. Every other nation is central bank–dominated and –controlled. This is why the US is able to utilize the power of economic sanctions all around the world. And the entire web has been opposing President Trump. Why would this be?

Some past presidents were all part of this same cabal. It spans the entire establishment of both of America's political parties. Often the players were pre-chosen and raised up from the elite circles and societies to hold these very positions. They served as front-men puppets to this Deep State globalist cabal. It didn't matter if they were Republican or Democrat; they would still push toward the same goals and plan. This is why we saw the same type of policy no matter who was in the White House.

Then something happened: God intervened. Just when the cabal was about to complete the globalist plan, further give up our rights and sovereignty, and solidify Agenda 2030 through various trade deals, treaties, and laws—just when the nail was about to be driven into the coffin, God heard the prayers of the saints and gave us a last-minute reprieve! He gave us a billionaire who was able to align with the patriots inside the government who wanted to stop the cabal and its sinister plan for our nation and world.

These patriots supported Donald Trump when he decided to run. He was the only one who was in a position to be able to answer this massive calling, the only one strong enough and wealthy enough to go against the cabal and circumvent their plan. This is why they hate him so much!

Hillary was supposed to win, but the patriots and the counter-coup mobilized and helped Donald Trump beat their rigged system. Hillary had the entire media, Hollywood, and Chinese apparatus working on her side. Her loss was a complete shock to them, which is why we saw the reactions we did. (And still are even today!)

Now the Deep State, media, Chinese Communists, Hollywood, and the entire one-party establishment system are still colluding to try and take Trump down. It's because he is the first president since Kennedy who is trying to dismantle their control. The Deep State has infiltrated every part of our society. If its proponents regain full power, they will make sure this never happens again. They will silence and crush the opposition. This is what is at stake! It is similar to pre-Nazi Germany. And trust me, the enemy is not Donald Trump!

Many Christian Never Trumpers are too busy focusing on Trump and all the corporate media's false narratives and psychological warfare operations to confuse and divide us so that we don't understand what is really at stake here.

But trust me on this. My four decades as a Christian journalist researching, observing, and reporting these matters have led me to understand the big picture here—when they do regain control and take power back, Christians will be target number one!

This time period could be closer than we think. God has given us a reprieve for a reason. His desire is that we repent and turn from our wicked ways. He wants the church to wake up and understand the true battle at hand. We are meant to lead culture and to be the head, not the tail. I believe if we were to repent, we could see a great revival in this nation. But again, we first need to understand that our problem is not Donald Trump; our problem is us. We need to see how far this nation and the church in this nation have strayed from our first love, Jesus Christ!

God has given us some time. What will we do with it? It may be shorter than we think. This is not business as usual. This is the time for us to rise up and be the church, the church God speaks about in His Word—one without spot or wrinkle (Eph. 5:27). We need to understand who the real enemies are. This is when revival will come!

> For our struggle is not against flesh and blood, but against the rulers, against the authorities, against the powers of this dark world and against the spiritual forces of evil in the heavenly realms.
>
> —Ephesians 6:12, niv

AFTERWORD

I OPENED THIS BOOK explaining that this short resource is a sequel to the most important book I've ever written, titled *God, Trump, and the 2020 Election*. I passionately believe the pandemic that started in China has impacted the entire world and will impact our election in ways we could not have imagined as recently as January, when the book was released. Had the COVID-19 pandemic happened while I was writing *God, Trump, and the 2020 Election*, I would have included much of the material you have just read.

God's Word says that greater is He who is in us than he who is in the world. (See 1 John 4:4.) God has a plan for America. This isn't just about electing a candidate but shifting things in America so there is a reprieve from the fast shift to the Left and godlessness. It is also giving an opportunity for what many are seeing as a coming Great Awakening, which is what our country (and the world) so desperately needs.

Now I need your help to tell your friends to buy *God, Trump, and the 2020 Election*. We need to get it in the hands of as many people as possible. Many Americans—even evangelical Christians—don't fully understand what is really going on, not only in the political and cultural realm but in the spiritual realm. You can get it most places where books are sold. Or check the website SteveStrangBooks.com to see how to get a copy signed by the author.

So, I hope you not only read *God, Trump, and the 2020 Election* but also buy copies for friends. To encourage the sale of large quantities, we list special discounted prices on the SteveStrangBooks.com website. Will you use my book to motivate others to support this president? So much is at stake that will affect your life and mine if he loses in November.

NOTES

INTRODUCTION

1. Joe Biden, "We are in the midst of a crisis with the coronavirus," Twitter, February 1, 2020, https://twitter.com/JoeBiden/status/12237279773613383 70?s=20.
2. "Donald Trump Charleston, South Carolina Rally Transcript—February 28, 2020," Rev, February 28, 2020, https://www.rev.com/blog/transcripts/donald-trump-charleston-south-carolina-rally-transcript-february-28-2020.
3. Gregg Re, "After Attacking Trump's Coronavirus-Related China Travel Ban as Xenophobic, Dems and Media Have Changed Tune," Fox News, April 1, 2020, https://www.foxnews.com/politics/dems-media-change-tune-trump-attacks-coronavirus-china-travel-ban.
4. Tal Axelrod, "Pelosi: Trump's Expanded Travel Ban Is 'Outrageous, Un-American' and Threatens 'Rule of Law,'" *Hill*, January 31, 2020, https://thehill.com/homenews/house/480991-pelosi-trumps-expanded-travel-ban-is-outrageous-un-american-and-threatens-rule.
5. Tim Hains, "Jesse Watters: Not Long Ago, Democrats Were Calling China Travel Ban 'Racist,'" RealClear Politics, April 5, 2020, https://www.realclearpolitics.com/video/2020/04/05/jesse_watters_not_long_ago_democrats_were_calling_china_travel_ban_racist.html.
6. Jon Levine, "Coronavirus Is 'Existential Threat' to Trump Re-election: GOP Insiders," *New York Post*, March 21, 2020, https://nypost.com/2020/03/21/coronavirus-is-existential-threat-to-trump-re-election-gop-insiders/.

CHAPTER 1

1. Mike Evans, "A Special Word From Dr. Mike Evans," Jerusalem Prayer Team, accessed April 24, 2020, http://pages.jerusalemprayerteam.org/2020-Coronavirus-Great-Awakening_2020-Coronavirus-Great-Awakening-LP-ALL.html?fbclid=IwAR2Sei68Jx14eI-I2BBTswgcU6N9dsZXGoagibsMRJJWJ9OKqk8U49UE9tA.
2. Jeremy Page, Wenxin Fan, and Natasha Khan, "How It All Started: China's Early Coronavirus Missteps," *Wall Street Journal*, March 6, 2020, https://www.wsj.com/articles/how-it-all-started-chinas-early-coronavirus-missteps-11583508932.
3. Brendon Hong, "China Arrested Doctors Who Warned About Coronavirus Outbreak. Now Death Toll's Rising, Stocks Are Plunging," Daily Beast, updated February 3, 2020, https://www.thedailybeast.com/china-arrested-doctors-who-warned-about-coronavirus-outbreak-now-death-tolls-rising-stocks-are-plunging.
4. J. Edward Moreno, "Stephen Moore: 'Economy Will Roar Back to Life' When Coronavirus Is Contained," Hill, March 8, 2020, https://thehill.com/homenews/

sunday-talk-shows/486472-stephen-moore-economy-will-roar-back-to-life-when-coronavirus-is.

5. Mark Moore, "Economist Stephen Moore Warns US Could Be Headed Toward a Great Depression," *New York Post*, April 5, 2020, https://nypost.com/2020/04/05/stephen-moore-warns-us-could-be-headed-toward-a-great-depression/.

6. Elaine Kamarck, "The Iranian Hostage Crisis and Its Effect on American Politics," Brookings, November 4, 2019, https://www.brookings.edu/blog/order-from-chaos/2019/11/04/the-iranian-hostage-crisis-and-its-effect-on-american-politics/.

7. Peter Beinart, "Trump Is Right About 9/11," *Atlantic*, October 19, 2015, https://www.theatlantic.com/politics/archive/2015/10/did-george-w-bush-do-all-he-could-to-prevent-911/411175/.

8. Michael Corkery and Annie Karni, "Trump Administration Restricts Entry Into U.S. From China," *New York Times*, updated February 10, 2020, https://www.nytimes.com/2020/01/31/business/china-travel-coronavirus.html.

9. Saim Saeed, "Trump's Europe Travel Ban Explained," Politico, updated March 13, 2020, https://www.politico.eu/article/coronavirus-donald-trump-europe-travel-ban-explained/.

10. Re, "After Attacking Trump's Coronavirus-Related China Travel Ban as Xenophobic, Dems and Media Have Changed Tune."

11. Catherine E. Shoichet, "93% of People Around the World Live in Countries With Coronavirus Travel Bans," CNN, April 1, 2020, https://www.cnn.com/travel/article/countries-with-travel-restrictions-coronavirus/index.html.

12. Peter Sullivan, "Fauci: 'Looks Like' US Deaths Will Be Lower Than Original Projection," *Hill*, April 8, 2020, https://thehill.com/homenews/coronavirus-report/491779-fauci-looks-like-us-deaths-will-be-lower-than-original-projection.

13. Brandt River, "Trump Battles the FDA Over Bill Gates's Breakthrough Discovery! Says 'This WILL NOT Be Banned, the American People Have a Right to Have Access to This,'" Business Insider, April 24, 2020, https://www.vox.com/2020/3/20/21188331/coronavirus-us-mexico-border-close.

14. Caitlin Oprysko and Susannah Luthi, "Trump Labels Himself 'a Wartime President' Combating Coronavirus," Politico, March 18, 2020, https://www.politico.com/news/2020/03/18/trump-administration-self-swab-coronavirus-tests-135590.

15. The White House, "President Trump Participates in an Easter Blessing With Bishop Harry Jackson," YouTube, April 10, 2020, https://www.youtube.com/watch?v=5ooC3v9j27o.

16. "Bishop Harry R. Jackson: Why Praying With Trump on Good Friday Was a Prophetic Act," Charisma Podcast Network, accessed April 25, 2020, https://www.charismapodcastnetwork.com/show/godtrumpandthe2020election/6f42b220-5b27-437a-9c3e-17c669d869c9.

17. "Bishop Harry R. Jackson: Why Praying With Trump on Good Friday Was a Prophetic Act," Charisma Podcast Network.

CHAPTER 2

1. Lance Wallnau, "Why I Believe Trump Is the Prophesied President," Charisma News, October 5, 2016, https://www.charismanews.com/politics/opinion/60378-why-i-believe-trump-is-the-prophesied-president.

2. Jonathan Sandys and Wallace Henley, *God and Churchill* (Carol Stream, IL: Tyndale, 2015), 80–81.

3. James Robison, "Faith and Prayer in the Oval Office: James Robison Speaks With Jack Graham," *Stream*, July 14, 2017, https://stream.org/faith-prayer-oval-office-james-robison-speaks-jack-graham/.

CHAPTER 3

1. Bruce Y. Lee, "Cases of COVID-19 Coronavirus Jumped Due to Change in Counting Method," *Forbes*, February 13, 2020, https://www.forbes.com/sites/brucelee/2020/02/13/new-coronavirus-covid-19-counting-method-leads-to-jump-in-cases-deaths/#530a289016af.

2. Tom Cotton, "Coronavirus and the Laboratories in Wuhan," *Wall Street Journal*, April 21, 2020, https://www.wsj.com/articles/coronavirus-and-the-laboratories-in-wuhan-11587486996.

3. John McCormack, "Cotton: Circumstantial Evidence 'Points Toward the Wuhan Labs,'" *National Review*, April 22, 2020, https://www.nationalreview.com/corner/cotton-circumstantial-evidence-points-toward-the-wuhan-labs/.

4. McCormack, "Cotton: Circumstantial Evidence 'Points Toward the Wuhan Labs.'"

5. Aylin Woodward, "The New Coronavirus Has Killed Nearly 3 Times as Many People in 8 Weeks as SARS Did in 8 Months. Here's How the 2 Outbreaks Compare," Business Insider, February 20, 2020, https://www.businessinsider.com/china-wuhan-coronavirus-compared-to-sars-2020-1.

6. Jane Parry, "Two Hong Kong Politicians Resign in Wake of SARS Report," *BMJ* 329, no. 7458 (July 17, 2004): 130, https://www.ncbi.nlm.nih.gov/pmc/articles/PMC478253/.

7. "Coronavirus: Hundreds in China Sign Petition Calling for Free Speech," Flipboard, February 11, 2020, https://flipboard.com/topic/calling/coronavirus-hundreds-in-china-sign-petition-calling-for-free-speech/f-fa9bcce10f%2Fscmp.com.

8. Mimi Lau, Echo Xie, and Guo Rui, "Coronavirus: Li Wenliang's Death Prompts Academics to Challenge Beijing on Freedom of Speech," *South China Morning Post*, February 12, 2020, https://www.scmp.com/news/china/politics/article/3050086/coronavirus-hundreds-chinese-sign-petition-calling-freedom?fbclid=IwAR2XocEo36ldcU-BCR9OAPcbr-onqrc3boK8RiAsllnvIlz_h0LKYWzc-I4.

9. Lisette Voytko, "'RIP Our Hero': Li Wenliang's Death Sparks Rare Outrage From Chinese Citizens Towards Government," *Forbes*, February 7, 2020, https://www. forbes.com/sites/lisettevoytko/2020/02/07/rip-our-hero-li-wenliangs-death-sparks-rare-outrage-from-chinese-citizens-towards-government/#74fea816565f.

CHAPTER 4

1. Dan Kopf and John Detrixhe, "A Coronavirus-Led Recession Could Hit Jobs for Young People and Minorities Hardest," Quartz, March 23, 2020, https:// qz.com/1822762/coronavirus-led-recession-in-us-could-hit-people-of-color-hardest/.

2. "Labor Force Statistics From the Current Population Survey," US Bureau of Labor Statistics, April 25, 2020, https://data.bls.gov/timeseries/LNS14000006.

3. Dan Diamond and Nancy Cook, "Trump Faces 'Black Swan' Threat to the Economy and Reelection," Politico, February 24, 2020, https://www.politico.com/ news/2020/02/24/trump-threat-coronavirus-reelection-economy-117272.

4. John Cassidy, "As the Coronavirus Spreads, Stocks Fall Again and the White House Frets About a Black Swan," *New Yorker*, February 25, 2020, https://www. newyorker.com/news/our-columnists/as-coronavirus-spreads-stocks-fall-again-and-the-white-house-frets-about-a-black-swan.

5. Ian Schwartz, "Maher: I'm 'Hoping' for 'a Crashing Economy' so We Can Get Rid of Trump, 'Bring on the Recession,'" RealClear Politics, June 9, 2018, https:// www.realclearpolitics.com/video/2018/06/09/maher_im_hoping_for_a_crashing_ economy_so_we_can_get_rid_of_trump_bring_on_the_recession.html.

6. Nassim Nicholas Taleb, *The Black Swan* (New York: Random House, 2007), xxii.

7. Sean McElwee, Jesse H. Rhodes, Brian F. Schaffner, and Bernard L. Fraga, "The Missing Obama Millions," *New York Times*, March 10, 2018, https://www. nytimes.com/2018/03/10/opinion/sunday/obamatrump-voters-democrats.html.

8. Philip Wegmann, "Trump Bets on More Black Support in 2020. (He Might Need It.)," RealClear Politics, June 7, 2019, https://www.realclearpolitics.com/ articles/2019/06/07/trump_bets_on_more_black_support_in_2020_he_might_ need_it.html; Asawin Suebsaeng, Sam Stein, and Lachlan Markay, "Trump's Plan to Stop Biden: Turn Black Voters Against Him," Daily Beast, May 30, 2019, https://www.thedailybeast.com/trumps-plan-to-stop-joe-biden-turn-black-voters-againsthim.

9. Janell Ross, "To Many Black Voters, Trump's Outreach Is More Showmanship Than Substance," NBC News, February 6, 2020, https://www.nbcnews. com/news/nbcblk/many-black-voters-trump-s-outreach-more-showmanship-substance-n1131601.

10. Richard North Patterson, "The Trump Virus Is Getting Worse," The Bulwark, April 3, 2020, https://thebulwark.com/38792-2/; Matt Wilstein, "Michael Moore to Colbert: We Need to 'Liberate' America From the 'Trump Virus,'" Daily Beast, April 22, 2020, https://www.thedailybeast.com/michael-moore-tells-stephen-colbert-we-need-to-liberate-america-from-the-trump-virus.

11. Candace Owens, "Candace Owens DESTROYS Leftist on Racism!," Facebook, August 9, 2018, https://www.facebook.com/ watch/?v=1799065083475533.

12. Wegmann, "Trump Bets on More Black Support in 2020. (He Might Need It.)."

CHAPTER 5

1. Re, "After Attacking Trump's Coronavirus-Related China Travel Ban as Xenophobic, Dems and Media Have Changed Tune."

2. Ian Schwartz, "Maher: I'm 'Hoping' for 'a Crashing Economy' So We Can Get Rid of Trump, 'Bring on the Recession,'" RealClear Politics, June 9, 2018, https://www.realclearpolitics.com/video/2018/06/09/maher_im_hoping_for_a_crashing_economy_so_we_can_get_rid_of_trump_bring_on_the_recession.html.

3. Michael Busler, "The Very Remarkable President Donald Trump," Townhall, April 13, 2020, https://townhall.com/columnists/michaelbusler/2020/04/13/the-very-remarkable-president-donald-trump-n2566739.

4. Busler, "The Very Remarkable President Donald Trump."

5. Cleta Mitchell, "The Real Coronavirus Chronology Shows Trump Was on Top of It While Biden Was Mocking the Danger," *Federalist*, March 31, 2020, https://thefederalist.com/2020/03/31/the-real-coronavirus-chronology-shows-trump-was-on-top-of-it-while-biden-was-mocking-the-danger/.

6. World Health Organization, "Preliminary investigations conducted by the Chinese authorities have found no clear evidence of human-to-human transmission of the novel #coronavirus (2019-nCoV) identified in #Wuhan, #China," Twitter, January 14, 2020, https://twitter.com/who/status/1217043229427761152?lang=en.

7. Berkeley Lovelace Jr. and William Feuer, "CDC Confirms First Human-to-Human Transmission of Coronavirus in US," CNBC, updated January 31, 2020, https://www.cnbc.com/2020/01/30/cdc-confirms-first-human-to-human-transmission-of-coronavirus-in-us.html.

8. Mitchell, "The Real Coronavirus Chronology Shows Trump Was on Top of It While Biden Was Mocking the Danger."

9. Mitchell, "The Real Coronavirus Chronology Shows Trump Was on Top of It While Biden Was Mocking the Danger."

10. Cortney O'Brien, "Trump Goes on a Tear Correcting Fake Coronavirus News," Townhall, April 12, 2020, https://townhall.com/tipsheet/cortneyobrien/2020/04/12/trump-goes-on-a-tear-correcting-fake-news-n2566785.

11. Donald J. Trump, "If the Fake News Opposition Party is pushing, with all their might, the fact that President Trump 'ignored early warnings about the threat,' then why did Media & Dems viciously criticize me when I instituted a Travel Ban on China?," Twitter, April 12, 2020, https://twitter.com/realdonaldtrump/status/1249437936539631616?lang=en.

12. Donald J. Trump, "Sorry Fake News, it's all on tape," Twitter, April 12, 2020, https://twitter.com/realdonaldtrump/status/1249470237726081030?lang=en.

13. DeAnna Lorraine, "Fauci is now saying that had Trump listened to the medical experts earlier he could've saved more lives," Twitter, April 12, 2020, https://twitter.com/DeAnna4Congress/status/1249457858686656512.

14. Reagan McCarthy, "Flip-Flop: Biden Now Backs Trump Travel Ban After Calling It 'Xenophobic,'" Townhall, April 3, 2020, https://townhall.com/tipsheet/reaganmccarthy/2020/04/03/biden-now-backs-trump-travel-ban-n2566339.

15. O'Brien, "Trump Goes on a Tear Correcting Fake Coronavirus News."

16. O'Brien, "Trump Goes on a Tear Correcting Fake Coronavirus News."

CHAPTER 6

1. Caleb Parke, "Pastors Object to NYC Mayor's Threat to Shut Down Churches," Fox News, April 1, 2020, https://www.foxnews.com/us/coronavirus-church-pastor-nyc-de-blasio-mayor-threat.

2. Terence P. Jeffrey, "Yes, Virginia's Governor Has Made It a Crime for More Than 10 People to Attend a Church Service," CNSNews.com, March 25, 2020, https://cnsnews.com/commentary/terence-p-jeffrey/yes-virginias-governor-has-made-it-crime-more-10-people-attend-church.

3. Liberty Counsel, "Are Churches Essential or Not?," Charisma News, April 8, 2020, https://www.charismanews.com/opinion/80675-are-churches-essential-or-not.

4. "Mayor Fischer Laments 'Painful' Time as Drive-Thru Church Services Won't Be Allowed for Holy Week," WDRB Media, April 7, 2020, https://www.wdrb.com/news/mayor-fischer-laments-painful-time-as-drive-thru-church-services-wont-be-allowed-for-holy/article_c7913fee-7909-11ea-afac-c77ed4014558.html.

5. Judge Justin R. Walker, "Temporary Restraining Order," US District Court Western District of Kentucky, April 11, 2020, https://www.courtlistener.com/recap/gov.uscourts.kywd.116558/gov.uscourts.kywd.116558.6.0.pdf.

6. Church of the Lukumi Balalu Aye Inc. v. City of Hialeah, 508 U.S. 520, 532 (1993) (quoting Bowen v. Roy, 476 U.S. 693, 703 (1986), as quoted in Walker, "Temporary Restraining Order."

7. Caleb Parke, "Louisville Mayor Reverses Drive-in Service Ban After Church Was Vandalized," Fox News, April 23, 2020, https://www.foxnews.com/us/coronavirus-louisville-mayor-church-service-ban-update.

8. "KY Court Rules for Louisville Church," Liberty Counsel, April 13, 2020, https://lc.org/newsroom/details/041320-ky-court-rules-for-louisville-church.

9. Godspeak Calvary Chapel, "What About Communion?" YouTube, April 3, 2020, https://www.youtube.com/watch?v=uEmO9Bp6txXE.

10. Alene Tchekmedyian and Carolyn Cole, "Thousand Oaks Councilman, a Pastor, Resigns, Says He'll Defy Coronavirus Order," Los Angeles Times, April 5, 2020, https://www.latimes.com/california/story/2020-04-05/thousand-oaks-councilman-resigns-communion-coronavirus-outbreak.

11. Alexander Smith, Pete Williams, Andrew Blankstein, et al., "Mass Shooting at Borderline Bar and Grill in Thousand Oaks, California," NBC Universal, November 8, 2018, https://www.nbcnews.com/news/us-news/shooting-reported-borderline-bar-grill-thousand-oaks-california-n933831.

12. "'60 Years, Gone:' As Woolsey Fire Survivors Struggle to Rebuild One Year Later, a Treatment Center Offers Hope," CBS Los Angeles, November 5, 2019, https://losangeles.cbslocal.com/2019/11/05/woolsey-fire-one-year/.

13. Michael Hernandez, "Outgoing Mayor Rob McCoy Feted at City Council Re-organization Meeting," Citizens Journal, December 4, 2019, https://www.citizensjournal.us/outgoing-mayor-rob-mccoy-feted-at-city-council-re-organization-meeting/.

14. Melissa Hurtado, "Thousand Oaks City Council Resignation," City of Thousand Oaks, April 5, 2020, https://www.toaks.org/Home/Components/News/News/8169/75.

15. "Pastors and Pro-Lifers Arrested While Abortion Industry Open to Spread Virus," Faith2Action, March 31, 2020, http://www.christiannewswire.com/news/7992683679.html?fbclid=IwAR1xzD1cGHOcdWYclELfAtPiGrHszh1P4AouHzkzni6yrhKlwTSUpcoDnWY.

16. "Pastors and Pro-Lifers Arrested While Abortion Industry Open to Spread Virus," Faith2Action.

17. Matti Stevenson, "Pro-Life Leaders Voice Alarm at Church Closures, Pastor's Arrest, While Abortion Facilities Remain Open in 47 States," Charisma News, April 2, 2020, https://www.charismanews.com/culture/80593-pro-life-leaders-voice-alarm-at-church-closures-pastor-s-arrest-while-abortion-facilities-remain-open-in-47-states.

18. Stevenson, "Pro-Life Leaders Voice Alarm at Church Closures, Pastor's Arrest, While Abortion Facilities Remain Open in 47 States."

19. "Ohio Attorney General Orders Abortion Providers to Halt Offering Procedure," Nexstar Broadcasting, March 21, 2020, https://www.nbc4i.com/news/local-news/ohio-attorney-general-orders-abortion-providers-to-halt-offering-procedure/.

20. "Health Care Professionals and Facilities, Including Abortion Providers, Must Immediately Stop All Medically Unnecessary Surgeries and Procedures to Preserve Resources to Fight COVID-19 Pandemic," Office of Texas Attorney General Ken Paxton, March 23, 2020, https://www.texasattorneygeneral.gov/news/releases/health-care-professionals-and-facilities-including-abortion-providers-must-immediately-stop-all.

21. Tal Axelrod, "Mississippi Governor Vows to Stop Abortions During Coronavirus Outbreak," *Hill*, March 24, 2020, https://thehill.com/homenews/state-watch/489328-mississippi-governor-vows-action-to-stop-abortions-during-coronavirus.

22. Dr. James Dobson, "Dr. Dobson Applauds Governors Greg Abbott and Mike DeWine for Halting Abortions in the Midst of the Pandemic, Calls on Other Governors to Follow Suit," Dr. James Dobson's Family Talk, March 26, 2020, https://www.drjamesdobson.org/about/latest-news/news-media/2020/03/26/dr.-dobson-applauds-governors-greg-abbott-and-mike-dewine-for-halting-abortions-in-the-midst-of-the-pandemic-calls-on-other-governors-to-follow-suit.

23. Ephrat Livni, "A New Abortion Debate Rages as Coronavirus Cripples the US," Quartz, April 2, 2020, https://qz.com/1830656/a-new-abortion-debate-rages-as-coronavirus-cripples-the-us/.

24. Stevenson, "Pro-Life Leaders Voice Alarm at Church Closures, Pastor's Arrest, While Abortion Facilities Remain Open in 47 States."

CHAPTER 7

1. Wesley J. Smith, "Nevada Governor Partially Bars Use of Malaria Drug for Coronavirus," National Review, March 25, 2020, https://www.nationalreview.com/corner/nevada-governor-bars-use-of-malaria-drug-for-coronavirus/.

2. J. Edward Moreno, "Democratic State Lawmaker Thanks Trump and Hydrochloroquine for Recovery From Coronavirus," Hill, April 7, 2020, https://thehill.com/homenews/state-watch/491612-democratic-state-rep-thanks-trump-and-hydroxychloroquine-for-recovery.

3. "Field Hospital Staffers Provide Around-the-Clock Care in New York's Central Park," Samaritan's Purse, April 15, 2020, https://www.samaritans-purse.org.uk/article/field-hospital-opens-in-new-york-citys-central-park/.

4. "Field Hospital Staffers Provide Around-the-Clock Care in New York's Central Park," Samaritan's Purse.

5. "Field Hospital Staffers Provide Around-the-Clock Care in New York's Central Park," Samaritan's Purse.

6. Gregory J. Holman, "Report: Assemblies of God World Missions Director Tests Positive for COVID-19," Springfield News-Leader, March 18, 2020, https://www.news-leader.com/story/news/local/missouri/2020/03/18/report-assemblies-god-missions-director-positive-covid-19/2872864001/.

CHAPTER 8

1. To request to read the full message, visit http://pages.jerusalemprayerteam.org/2020-Coronavirus-Great-Awakening_2020-Coronavirus-Great-Awakening-LP-ALL.html?fbclid=IwAR2Sei68Jx14eI-I2BBTswgcU6N9dsZXGoagibsMRJJWJ9OKqk8U49UE9tA.

2. Caleb Parke, "Christian Pastor Shawn Bolz: 'Lord Showed Me the End of the Coronavirus,'" Fox News, March 3, 2020, https://www.foxnews.com/faith-values/coronavirus-christian-pastor-shawn-bolz.

3. To listen to that podcast, visit Stephen Strang, "Why Shawn Bolz Prophesied the Coronavirus Is About to End Despite Public Panic," Strang Report, March

9, 2020, https://www.charismanews.com/opinion/80249-why-shawn-bolz-prophesied-the-coronavirus-is-about-to-end-despite-public-panic.

4. Michael Le Page and Debora Mackenzie, "Could the New Coronavirus Really Kill 50 Million People Worldwide?," New Scientist, February 11, 2020, https://www.newscientist.com/article/2233085-could-the-new-coronavirus-really-kill-50-million-people-worldwide/.

5. Emily Czachor, "Dr. Fauci Says U.S. Coronavirus Deaths Could Be Far Less Than Predicted, but Cautions Against Loosening Social Distancing Restrictions," *Newsweek*, April 9, 2020, https://www.newsweek.com/dr-fauci-says-us-coronavirus-deaths-could-far-less-predicted-cautions-against-loosening-1497120.

Chapter 9

1. John Paul Jackson, *7 Days Behind the Veil: Throne Room Meditations* (Lewisville, TX: Streams Publishing House, 2008).

2. Chuck D. Pierce, *The Passover Prophecies* (Lake Mary, FL: Charisma House, 2020), https://www.amazon.com/Passover-Prophecies-Realigning-Hearts-Nations/dp/1629999075/ref=tmm_pap_swatch_0?_encoding=UTF8&qid=1587932402&sr=8-1.

3. Pierce, The Passover Prophecies.

4. Pierce, The Passover Prophecies.

5. Eleanor Albert, "Christianity in China," Council on Foreign Relations, October 11, 2018, https://www.cfr.org/backgrounder/christianity-china.

6. Cal Pierce, "WE, AS THE BODY OF CHRIST, SPEAK TO THIS MOUNTAIN OF CORONAVIRUS…," Facebook, March 12, 2020, https://www.facebook.com/cal.pierce.102/posts/3066110123434450.

7. Stephen Strang, "Marco Rubio Holds Urgent COVID-19 Briefing for Pastors," Charisma News, March 24, 2020, https://www.charismanews.com/opinion/80453-marco-rubio-holds-urgent-covid-19-briefing-for-pastors.

8. Stephen Strang, "Prophetic Dream Reveals What God Is Saying About Trump and the Coronavirus," Charisma News, March 25, 2020, https://www.charismanews.com/opinion/80473-prophetic-dream-reveals-what-god-is-saying-about-trump-and-the-coronavirus.

9. Strang, "Prophetic Dream Reveals What God Is Saying About Trump and the Coronavirus."

10. "United States Coronavirus Cases," Worldometer, accessed April 28, 2020, https://www.worldometers.info/coronavirus/country/us/.

11. Jeffry Bartash, "Jobless Claims Jump Another 4.4 million—26 Million Americans Have Lost Their Jobs to the Coronavirus," MarketWatch Inc., April 23, 2020, https://www.marketwatch.com/story/jobless-claims-jump-another-44-million-25-million-americans-have-lost-their-jobs-to-the-coronavirus-2020-04-23.

12. Stephen Strang, "Prophetic Dream Reveals What God Is Saying About Trump and the Coronavirus," *Strang Report*, accessed April 28, 2020, https://www.

charismamag.com/blogs/the-strang-report/44799-prophetic-dream-reveals-what-god-is-saying-about-trump-and-the-coronavirus.

CHAPTER 10

1. Blue Letter Bible, s.v. "kairos," accessed April 25, 2020, https://www.blueletterbible.org/lang/Lexicon/Lexicon.cfm?strongs=G2540&t=KJV.

2. Vocabulary.com, s.v. "opportunity," accessed April 26, 2020, https://www.vocabulary.com/dictionary/opportunity.

3. Vocabulary.com, s.v. "opportunity," accessed April 26, 2020, https://www.vocabulary.com/dictionary/opportunity.

4. For more information about The Return, visit https://www.thereturnwebsite.org/index.php.